PRAISE FOR

GO WEST, YOUNG MAN . . .

"We all have things we have done that were fun and exciting, and we all have things we wish we had done. I wish I could have been on this trip with these guys! What a fun book! What a fun trip, and Gary Spillers takes us with him by telling his stories in a humorous and Southern-fried way."

—Phillip Fulmer
College Football Analyst and
Former Football Coach, Tennessee Volunteers

"Read your book and thought it was laugh out loud great. Can't wait for your next one!"

—Linda Head
General Manager, Dogwood Retirement Community

"I really enjoyed the book, and after reading it I left my copy in my 87-year-old father's car by mistake. He found the book and started reading a few pages, but he didn't put it down until he had finished it! Later, he told me he liked it so much he couldn't stop reading it, and then he said, 'That Spillers boy is a wild one, isn't he?'"

—Johnny Cowart
President, Johnny Cowart Agency

"I read your book in two nights. My wife kept asking me what the heck was so funny?!?"

—Bob Butterworth
President, Bob Butterworth State Farm Insurance

"Gary, here's the check for your book, although it's worth twice the price!! Enjoyed it immensely!!"

—W.E. (Ed) Robinson III
Retired Executive

GO WEST, YOUNG MAN
...*BUT DON'T COME BACK!*

MOSTLY TRUE TALES FROM A
SOUTHERN BOY'S TRAVELS

GARY SPILLERS

Vabella Publishing

Vabella Publishing
P.O. Box 1052
Carrollton, Georgia 30112

Second Edition

Manufactured in the United States of America

13-digit ISBN 978-0-9712204-9-2

Disclaimer: If the reader thinks that some of the author's slang is incorrect King's English, the reader is more than likely correct. But he or she will just have to live with it 'cause it sounds good to the author who just "don't know no better!"

Special thanks to all the editors of this book: Rebecca Teaff, Staci Mae Spillers, Jackie Spillers Johnson, Deborah Fite, Gloria Garrett, Carmen Whitesell, and Virginia Bell. This bunch of good-looking women took what was basically an assault on the English language and molded it into an interesting and enjoyable, fun read.

11 10 9 8 7 6 5 4 3 2

Library of Congress Cataloging-in-Publication Data

Spillers, Gary, 1948-
  Go west, young man . . . but don't come back!: mostly true tales from a southern boy's travels / Gary Spillers.
      p. cm.
   ISBN 978-0-9712204-9-2 (pbk.)
1. West (U.S.)--Description and travel. 2. West (U.S.)--Humor. 3. Southern States--Description and travel. 4. Southern States--Humor. 5. Spillers, Gary, 1948---Travel--West (U.S.) 6. Spillers, Gary, 1948---Travel--Southern States. 7. Milledgeville (Ga.)--Biography. 8. Atlanta (Ga.)--Biography. I. Title.
  F595.3.S69 2011
  978--dc22
                              2011009856

For Etta Mae Spillers

This book is dedicated to my "Bible-toting" mother, Etta Mae Spillers, the rock of the Spillers family who is 86 years young and still good-looking. Like the energizer bunny, she just keeps on ticking. Etta Mae still drives herself all over town and to church and the beauty shop every week.

Even though I have been a maverick many times in my life, she has always stood beside me and believed in me all the way.

I never suspected my mother knew any curse words, nor was I aware of her keen sense of humor until one day, as a young teenager, I was in a bad mood and was whining about anything and everything.

Mom reproached me, "Bruce, I think you have a bad case of 'opterectitus!'"

"What's that, Mom?" I asked.

"It's a condition caused by your optical gland getting mixed up with your rectal gland, and it gives you a shitty outlook on life!"

I love you, Mom, and I hope you enjoy "most" of the book!

Special recognition for the creation of this book also goes to my siblings: "Queen" Jackie Johnson, Sue Ellen Brack, and Larry "Snake" Spillers. Etta Mae built this ship, but my fellow mates have all helped keep it afloat and sailing in the right direction. They are one of the groups that actually did want me to come back. (I think?)

PROLOGUE

My name is Gary Spillers. I'm from Milledgeville, Georgia, where my name is pronounced Gay-Ree! I lived in Atlanta for several years where I was much more sophisticated. I learned to sip champagne and taste wine with more worldly colleagues, instead of chugging beers at happy hour with Ed "Dodo" Hollis and the boys down at THE Milledgeville Pool Room. My name had even been "yankeefied" from the Atlanta exposure and is now pronounced Gaa-ry.

This book is written about and for people who pronounce my name properly. And that is Gay-Ree. Not that some of you Yankees out there won't love these tales; I am sure you will. But it's just different living in the South. When you meet my friends, Lionel Ed Rainey, Jack Maddox, "Cool Head" Hedrick, "Slimey" Spikes, "Alert" Eddie Powell, J. "Moe" Gillespie, and "Red-Headed" Shelly Centers, you will see for yourself that these guys and girls approached problems and opportunities . . . shall we say, differently.

I graduated from Troy State University in Troy, Alabama, in December 1970. I attended Troy on a tryout football scholarship—a humble start, but I worked and took advantage of it to become an All-Conference linebacker and team captain my senior year. Many of the characters in this book are guys and girls I met at Troy and the other two colleges I attended.

A job interviewer at Troy once asked if I enjoyed being a marketing major. I told him that my real major was football, and they threw in the marketing degree as a bonus. He thought that was hilarious. Hell, I was being serious!

I landed a job out of Troy with the textile giant Deering-Milliken in Union, South Carolina, but I ended up hating it and left after only six months. I returned home to Milledgeville, Georgia, and began framing houses with my best friend from high school, Larry Eady. This move guided me indirectly into real estate brokerage where I have been working over the last forty years.

In November 1976, I headed west to see the "left coast": first, possibly to find a better place to live and seek career opportunities along the way; and second, to contemplate my unstable relationship with my girlfriend, Cheryl Petros. Plus, I needed a change of scenery and time to myself to make decisions about my future.

Being a small-town Georgia boy, I couldn't imagine how any other state could compare with mine. Georgia is graced with diverse topography—oceanfronts, mountains, gorgeous lakes, rivers, and forests—and it boasts an international city where a short drive to the airport could get you anywhere on the world map. Yet, in the stories that follow, you will see I was pleasantly surprised and humored by what the West had to offer.

The trip that began in Atlanta would take me through most of the West, including treks through Missouri, Kansas, Wyoming, Colorado, Utah, Montana, California, Mexico,

Nevada, Arizona, Texas, and, eventually, back to the good ole Southeast.

Imagine a simple southerner being exposed to the bizarre nuances of the "Wild West" while traveling in a suspect 1967 Chevrolet. Then add Lindy, a young lady with whom I had a brief, but hot romance a few months earlier, and things get a little more interesting. The only way to break those long, uncomfortable silences as we roared westward was to entertain Lindy, my "co-pilot," with the tall tales of my college escapades and life just after college.

So pour yourself a glass of wine or pop the top on a cold beer, and let's see what happens!

TABLE OF CONTENTS

Prologue

The Green Pig and its westward-seeking occupants leave Atlanta and head north through Western Tennessee—Chattanooga, Nashville, and Clarksville—the edge of Kentucky, the western side of Indiana, and on to St. Louis, Missouri.

Leaving St. Louis and the Gateway to the West behind in the dust, the Green Pig and its well-rested travelers take a western bearing on I-70 that will take them through Columbia, Missouri, then on to Kansas City, Missouri. The great state of Kansas is next, with its endless supply of wheat fields and prairie land, followed by an interesting welcome to the magnificent state of Colorado and eventually, Colorado Springs.

Epilogue

GO WEST, YOUNG MAN
...*BUT DON'T COME BACK!*

CHAPTER ONE

"Gary Spillers, if you think for one damn minute that I am going to load my luggage into that 'deathtrap' for a 6,000-mile, cross-country trip, you are CRAZY! Where's the Mercedes? This is a joke, isn't it?" exclaimed Lindy Stevens, my traveling partner, upon seeing the "Green Pig" for the first time, which was to be our mode of transportation to the West Coast and back . . . hopefully.

In October 1976, my friend Tommy Arrington had once again bailed on our plan to travel out West and see the "left" side of the country. One of our friends from Atlanta, Jenna Stubbs, had moved to Aspen, Colorado, in the spring. The "ski resort" had just come into vogue and was one of the coolest places on the planet to be. Tommy had visited Jenna in the summer and returned with glowing stories about how cool—no pun intended—Aspen was. Tommy and I had planned to go back in the fall and get jobs out there and work through the ski season.

The love of my life, Cheryl Petros, had abandoned me and her Atlanta modeling career a couple months earlier for a job as a flight attendant with Northwest Orient, an airline based in Minneapolis, Minnesota. I endured an uncomfortable and heart-tugging drive with her all the way from Atlanta to Minneapolis. It was the longest, most painful trip I ever took. Cheryl had earlier graduated from Western Kentucky and, in a short period, acquired success as one of the top models in Atlanta. We vowed to "be there for each other," thinking we were in love. But when I left her in the airport in Minneapolis to fly back to Atlanta, I knew it would never be the same. It couldn't be. We would see each other once or twice a month for a couple of days, and that would be it! This was a perfect time for me to travel and get some thinking done about what I wanted to do with the rest of my life.

The trip out West seemed to be the perfect medicine at that time. Even though I knew I was a big boy and could handle myself, I still had serious reservations about this trip.

Would the "Green Pig" really make it to the West Coast and, more important, would it make it back? Would my money run out and, if it did, what would I do? Would there be interesting work out there for me? What did Cheryl really think about my traveling out West, and did she even care? With all these uncertainties, I was thinking maybe I should just cancel the trip and go back to work somewhere in Atlanta . . . . Naah! I didn't think so!

Tommy and I had previously discussed leaving in September, but those plans fell through. October arrived, and he still wasn't ready. But The West was calling me! You hear all these descriptions of places, but until you visit them yourself, you really don't know what to expect. Kinda' like the time a buddy of mine recommended a striptease club in New Orleans. Upon visiting said club, we were thoroughly enjoying ourselves until we realized all the dancers were men. It just wasn't the same!

I told Tommy if he wasn't ready to go in November, I was going by myself. Of course, he didn't believe me, but as far as I was concerned, come hell or high water, I was going out west in November!

A couple of days later, I was sitting in a bar talking to a former girlfriend, Lindy Stevens, and telling her all about my frustrating situation. Wild Cherry's "Play that Funky Music" blared in the background, and a billow of cigarette smoke rose from the depths of the bar, leaving a putrid, choking smell surrounding us as we chatted. Unable to contain her excitement, Lindy piped up and said, "I'll go with you. I have always wanted to see the 'Wild, Wild West.'"

"Whoa there, sweet thang," I said. "The reason I have been waiting on Tommy is mostly monetary. We were going to split the cost of the trip down the middle."

"That's okay," said Lindy. "I have just been laid off from my teacher's job until next spring. I am getting severance pay, so I can afford to split the expenses with you fifty-fifty. It sounds like fun! When do you want to leave?"

I was a little stunned that Lindy wanted to go. But she was serious. She also mentioned that she had a former roommate then living in Colorado Springs who would put us up for a couple of days. So Lindy was ready to leave almost immediately—with or without Tommy. Even though I knew Tommy wouldn't show, I told her we still would have to wait for his decision. The other matter we had to deal with was that this had to be a strictly "platonic" trip; there would be no sex—a pledge I didn't think Lindy would uphold, especially when she had to sleep in close quarters with a "hunk" like me.

Lindy really loved my slick, red 300 Mercedes Benz two-door coupe. After our meeting about the trip, I had failed to mention to her that I was selling that car and we would instead be traveling in a car I had traded my roommate a used color TV set for . . . a green, 1967 Chevy Impala (nicknamed the "Green Pig"). This car was not a looker, but it had a fantastic running, Chevy 283 engine in it, and it was large and in excellent road condition. Until, that is, I left it in the parking lot of a local public park on Halloween night. At that time, I was refereeing youth football games to get extra cash together for the pending trip. When I went to retrieve the vehicle the next morning, it was missing in action. After checking with the local forest rangers, I discovered that the car had been "rolled," not with toilet paper, but literally rolled over on its top by local teenage gangs looking for thrills on Halloween night.

The damage was severe, and I had no insurance on the vehicle. With the windshield shattered and the roof a little caved in, I managed to drive it down to Milledgeville where my good friend "Trip" Bradford, body shop man extraordinaire, agreed to fix it for a couple hundred bucks and a fifth of Jack Daniel's. He literally glued the windshield back in place, yucky black ooze dripping from the edges, and kicked the roof of the car back close to its original position. With a new set of Michelins, a brake job, and an oil change, the Green Pig was back on the road again.

After the unexpected expenses from the cost of repairing the car, I was down to a low point in cash on hand. I had already left my real estate job at Buckhead Brokers. (That was back when Buckhead Brokers had only five agents, so my leaving them cut it back to four. The company was sold and caught fire after I left and became one of the biggest real estate companies in Atlanta.) I mustered a few odd jobs to get the money together for the trip. A couple of days before we were supposed to leave, I went to my bank to check on my available cash at the 24-hour teller and found an additional 800 dollars! The bank must have made a mistake. Wow! With the additional "manna from heaven," I now had enough cash to go.

The Green Pig was already a little rusty and the paint was fading, but the car ran like a test car for NASCAR. What more could you ask for? Well, one thing would be Lindy's approval. When I arrived at her apartment to pick her up for the trip and she saw the Green Pig for the first time, she lost it!

I had some selling to do, which I did, and finally convinced Lindy that as much as I thought of myself, I would never put either of us in harm's way with an unsafe vehicle. Finally, I convinced her to go, and we hit the road. Westward Hoooo!

Well, it was more like Northwestward Hoooo! Our route would take us north through Chattanooga and Nashville, up through the edge of Indiana, and then on to St. Louis, Missouri, via I-64. A friend of mine from Milledgeville was dating a lady by the name of Gayle Johnson from St. Louis who happened to be in Milledgeville the weekend I went down to pick up the "repaired" Green Pig. When I told her our trip would probably take us through St. Louis, Gayle offered to let us spend the night at her apartment and show us the town.

As the Green Pig was humming along I-75 between Chattanooga and Nashville, with the Bee Gees harmonizing in the background, Lindy reminded me of my promise to share some of my stories with her. I gladly obliged.

"Do you remember the grand opening weekend of T.G.I. Friday's first restaurant in Atlanta?" I queried. She said that she hadn't, but if it was all that special, she wanted to hear more about it.

I said okay, but my main thought at that moment was that Friday's was where I had met Cheryl. After we were dating for a while, we were back in the restaurant one night imbibing some strong spirits when Cheryl excused herself to go to the ladies' room. A few minutes later, I decided that was a good idea for me, too, so I retired to the men's room only to find Cheryl, standing with her hands on her hips in the middle of the room. I blurted, "Cheryl, what are you doing in the men's room?"

She retorted, "Gary, you are mistaken. YOU are in the ladies' room, and I know that for a fact, because I just left the men's room!" Oh, the fun we had!

The name of my first tale is "We Have a First at Friday's."

WE HAVE A FIRST AT FRIDAY'S

During the spring of 1974 in Atlanta, the latest hot singles bar, T.G.I. Friday's, was added to the scene in a new shopping center called The Prado, which was located near the intersection of Roswell Road and I-285.

The early '70s was a magical time to live in Atlanta. Being single and cool in this southern metropolis was about as good as it gets, especially when new singles watering holes stocked with gorgeous southern ladies were opening on a regular basis.

The Atlanta Raft Race down the Chattahoochee River past Riverbend Apartments was the singles social event of the year. *Time Magazine* featured Riverbend Apartment's pool scene on its front cover, proclaiming singles life in Atlanta as tops in the nation.

In the early '70s, most of the singles bars were stretched along, or not far from, Peachtree and Roswell Roads. Singles frequented popular places like the famous Harrison's; the Brave-Falcon; the Second Sun; the Chalet; the then, now, and forever popular dance club, Johnny's Hideaway; The Brandy House; Ray's on the River; McGruder's; Gerald's; Penrod's; and now T.G.I. Friday's, with Daddy's Money opening soon after. Oddly, these bars and watering holes were responsible for a reduction in the number of singles in Atlanta, as many of the singles met their future mates in these places and eventually ended up getting married. On the other hand, these "dens of iniquity" were just as responsible for causing an equal number of divorces. In the jungle, it's called herd stabilization.

****

Though there were no lions for the ladies to fear, in and around the "watering holes" of Atlanta . . . there were plenty of SHARKS! These sharks weren't just men, as my good friend and fellow shark Andy Smith discovered one night. Andy's "go-to bar" (defined as the place you go to pick up a woman when all hope is lost at your other haunts) was the Brave-Falcon. So Andy went to the Brave-Falcon rather late one night and, sure enough, he picks up this lady and goes home with her.

The next morning, Andy noticed a hump at the bottom of the bed. Upon checking it out, he saw it was the head of the lady's little boy. "Mommy, who is this?" the boy said, pointing to Andy.

"Oh, Honey, this is Uncle Andy," the mother said.

The kid continued to stare at Andy, and then said, "Well, what happened to Uncle George that was here before him?"

****

Friday's also brought a new and special tradition to the singles of North Atlanta: the Saturday morning Champagne Brunch, featuring Eggs Benedict, Eggs Sardou, and Friday's delicious Bloody Marys. Most of the single rednecks didn't know what the hell these exotic egg recipes were at first, but they learned to love them fast. If you didn't get to Friday's early on Saturday, you usually didn't get a table until later in the day, which was fine with most of the singles because it was awful tough to get up early on Saturday morning after "runnin' a good one" all night on Friday night at some of the aforementioned places of distinction. Amazingly, all of this early popularity occurred before the official grand opening of the restaurant.

When the Saturday morning of the Grand Opening for T.G.I. Friday's came, the Atlanta weather couldn't have been better. It was a gorgeous Georgia spring day, close to time for The Masters, and the dogwoods and azaleas were in full bloom. Along with Friday's grand opening, The Prado Shopping Center was also having a promotion featuring the Atlanta Polo Club, with all the riders and their horses decked out in silks and mallets, parading around the parking lot. I guess spring and horses go together in the South. The Atlanta Steeplechase was a hot ticket for singles in the early '70s, and the game of polo was becoming popular as well. Not to mention the spring Derby parties, usually hosted by lovely southern ladies with their best mint julep recipes.

At the time of the much-anticipated restaurant grand opening, Friday's employed a host/DJ type who announced to waiting guests when their tables were ready and often bantered with them, the bartenders, and the wait staff. We had anointed the host "Freddy Friday." Freddy was genuinely quick-witted and fun and kept everyone in a good mood during the brunch.

On opening day, Freddy Friday was keen on announcing all the "firsts." It was the first official grand opening of a T.G.I. Friday's in Atlanta; it was the first promotion of The Prado Shopping Center; and, of course, it was the first promotion that featured the Atlanta Polo Club in their parking lot.

Between the breaks of seating and announcing guests' table availability, Freddy Friday got a bright idea that he thought was really cool. He went outside and talked one of the polo players into bringing his horse inside the restaurant. The horse was brought through the lobby into the front of the restaurant onto a dining area with a brick and hardwood floor, just before some steps that led to an elevated bar. You can only imagine how crowded the new restaurant was on grand opening day packed with drunks and party animals, devouring their Eggs Benedict and Sardou, champagne, and Bloody Marys.

The polo horse, though a little timid at first, was settling down as people were coming over and petting him, making both horse and rider feel comfortable and welcome. Upon being convinced that he had made a brilliant marketing decision by bringing the horse and rider inside the restaurant, Freddy Friday grabbed his microphone and announced, "We have a first at Friday's! We have a live polo horse and his rider inside of Friday's!"

Everyone cheered the horse and the rider. That's about the time it happened . . . some inebriated knucklehead accidentally (I think?) dropped a large, glass beer mug from the elevated bar. It smashed very close to the horse's feet, exploding on the hardwood floor with a tremendous "BANG" and shocking the horse into a panic mode. All four legs shot out from under the horse at once. As the horse struggled to steady its legs and maintain some traction, it spun around in a circle and sprayed horse manure all over the dining tables and the patrons who were seated close by!

Finally righting himself, the horse bolted out the door, dragging his rider, who was helpless in trying to control the spooked animal. Both horse and rider were last seen in the parking lot, dodging traffic—possibly headed back to the polo fields somewhere up in Roswell.

Do you think all of this flustered Freddy Friday? Why hell, no! As the horse bolted out through the front doors of the restaurant, dragging his rider and fertilizing everything and everybody in its path, Freddy Friday grabbed his microphone once more and boomed excitedly, "WE NOW HAVE ANOTHER FIRST AT FRIDAY'S!" The whole restaurant exploded with thunderous applause . . . well, except the people sitting in range of the recently departed, riderless, poop-spraying polo horse!

Lindy laughed so hard at the story that her body jolted forward, and she hit her head on the dashboard of the car.

"Actually," she said, "my favorite part of that story was how the tables got turned on that shark Uncle Andy." And all those bars you talked about . . . some of them I know about, and some I've never heard of."

"Have you ever heard of a place called the Domino Lounge downtown on Peachtree?" I asked.

Lindy said no, but she placed a finger near her mouth, listening with great interest.

"The Domino Lounge is one of the oldest strip joints, (or 'titty bars' as my good friend Wilbur Bell used to call them) in Atlanta and is an important part of my next story."

One of the year's hit songs, "Disco Lady" by Johnnie Taylor, boomed from the Green Pig's radio, setting a perfect backdrop for the next tale I call "The Ride." This story was about finding myself in a reincarnation of the fictional town of Mayberry from the popular '60s sitcom *The Andy Griffith Show*. Outside the car window, I could see stretches of tranquil Tennessee farmland and other picturesque spots that were virtually invisible on the U.S. map.

THE RIDE

Every time I see a Gwinnett County license plate, I can't help but think of Mayberry and the trip back to Atlanta from a snow-skiing adventure in the North Carolina mountains. I don't remember the actual name of the town because I was mentally thinking I really was in Mayberry.

The place harbored all the important amenities of small-town life: a hospitable barber shop, a county courthouse set smack in the center of the town, good ole' boys sitting on the front porches, and southern belles gossiping and window shopping near the storefronts. It truly felt like I had landed on the set of *Andy Griffith*, with Barney, Goober, and the other characters.

I don't know whether it was because of Barney Fife, the stumbling, bumbling deputy, or Opie Taylor, the sheriff's young son (whom everyone said I looked like in my younger years), but this was by far my favorite TV show of all time.

As I was admiring Mayberry, I noticed my car was low on gas and whipped into a local gas station to fill up. The service station was a throwback to the early '60s, with glass-globed gas pumps that dinged as each gallon was pumped. Not to mention the station attendant who not only pumped your gas, but checked your oil and washed your windshield as a courtesy without your having to request it.

When I got out of the car, I noticed a gas station attendant I'll call Goober, standing nearby with an aloof look on his face, his baseball cap and grease rag hanging out of his rear pocket. He was wearing penny loafers with a penny in each shoe.

"Filler up?" He asked as he half danced and half strode toward my car.

"You don't have to check the oil because there ain't any in there!" I said.

We both laughed and immediately bonded. Goober reached for my gas cap when he noticed my car tag said Gwinnett County.

"Gwin-nett County. Where is that?"

"Oh, it's Atlanta," I said. "I live in Cobb Coun . . ."

He interrupted. "Did you say Etlanter? Are you from Etlanter, sho nuff?"

"Yeah . . ." I started, but my friend interrupted again.

"I been to Etlanter," he said.

He twisted his head around like an owl as if shying away from what he was about to tell me. I could tell his Atlanta story was sure to come.

Every small-town person in the Southeast has an Atlanta story. Some are good; some are bad. But when a small-town person finds out that you are from Atlanta, you are going to hear their Atlanta story. A lady who worked for me in South Carolina had a wreck in Atlanta on her way through Atlanta to Florida and another on her way back from Florida. She will not go within 100 miles of Atlanta at any time of year. Another old codger sitting outside of a similar country gas station down in South Georgia once found out I was from Atlanta. As he spat tobacco juice on the ground, he

Go West, Young Man

declared, "Et . . . lanter . . . shit . . . I wouldn't go up thar and git it, if they give it to me!"

Twisting his head around more than before, to really be sure no one was listening, as the gallons dinged away, Goober began his Etlanter story. I could tell this was going to be a good one.

"You ever heard of a place called the Domino Lounge?" he asked. I laughed. As a kid from Milledgeville, I knew this place. The Domino Lounge was one of the first strip clubs I ever visited. During the '60s, it was one of the top gentlemen's clubs on Peachtree Street. I just nodded my head and confided to my new friend that I had been there before.

On cue, he proceeded. "Me and my buddy Earl was a drinkin' sto' bought whiskey one day when we decided to take a ride. We was going to take a ride down to the big city to check out the scenery, if you know what I mean?"

He topped off the tank and began the ritual cleaning of the windshield while keeping me spellbound with his country-smart wit.

"We done heard about this place called the Domino Lounge, and that is exactly where we headed. SON! Them was the purtiest girls I ever saw in my life. They were a dancing, shaking, and gyrating around. And all of 'em was butt nekkid!" (The difference between being naked and nekkid, as defined by the late Lewis Grizzard, is that naked meant that you didn't have clothes on, but nekkid meant you didn't have clothes on and you were up to something!)

"I could tell one of them named Betty was taking a liking to me. I was makin' plans in my mind how I could move down to this place so's I could do this every day. Boy! We was a having ourselves one of them real good times! We had been in there about an hour or so when, directly, Earl rolled his eyes toward the ceiling, and this strange look done overtook his face . . . then he done bolted upright and looked over at me and said, 'Paul, what if we'd be a sittin' here when the Lord comes?'"

After a silent interlude, I had to know what happened.

"What do you think happened? said Goober. "We got the hell out of there and drove all the way back up here. And you know what? We ain't been back, neither! That will be $12.75, please."

"What an ending!" Lindy exclaimed.

"I bet those goobers up there have told that story a million times around that service station, but only when nobody was a lookin' of course.

"Tell me, Gary, you have been around Atlanta for a while now. What apartment community is the best for singles?"

"Well, everybody defines the top three as Riverbend, Treetops, and Palisades, but I think that's mostly hype. Cumberland Apartments over by Vining's is a great spot. I have several buddies who live there. Then there is The Lakes, which flight attendants love. In my opinion, it's hard to go wrong if you can find a nice, clean apartment complex anywhere from Roswell Road back west to just past the intersection of I-75 and I-285. Singles just love this part of Atlanta.

"One of the area's worst traffic problems was the single-lane bridge crossing the Chattahoochee River at Riverbend Apartments. This single-lane bridge worked fine as long as everyone was courteous and waited his turn, but when some hothead, drunk or sober, tried to force the issue, all hell broke loose! This was a real problem on weekends when Riverbend hosted large parties for singles.

"If you want to know my favorite apartment complex in this area, it is by far a place called Shadowood located on Powers Ferry Road."

SHADOWOOD

In the spring of 1974, I lived in an apartment complex in Atlanta named Shadowood located on Powers Ferry Road just north of 1-285 and the Chattahoochee River. Shadowood was just down the road from the infamous Riverbend Apartments, which had just been rated by *Time Magazine* as one of the hottest singles spots in the country.

My roommate at Shadowood was Peter Hendricks. Peter was a divorced guy, partly bald, and aside from that, a Yankee who worked for a bill collections company. So what was a young, single, wild-ass guy like me doing living with a conservative guy like this?

When I visited Shadowood Apartments for the first time, I was shopping for another one-bedroom apartment that would be cheaper than the one I currently had at Riverbend. Melanie Chapman, the previous Miss Atlanta pageant winner, was my leasing agent and lived next door to Peter's apartment.

Melanie said, "I think I have something you may be interested in. My next-door neighbor, who has a two-bedroom, two and one-half bath townhouse with a fireplace, has told me that if I found a sharp person who would be a good potential roommate, to show his apartment. He will split the cost with you, and you will have your own private bedroom and bath. Now, Gary, Peter is a little older and more conservative than you. But he travels all the time, and when he is home, he usually stays with his girlfriend, Judy, who lives down in the married section of Shadowood. And one more thing, I will be your next-door neighbor!"

"Wow." I said. "I'm not much on roommates, but let's take a look."

It was love at first site . . . the apartment I mean! An abundance of hard liquor, beer, and wine filled every corner of the place! Coincidently, Peter was a senior vice president for one of the largest collection companies in the country. He was in charge of the Southeast region and had an unlimited expense account. When he and his salespeople entertained, most of the extra booze would end up back at his apartment.

So I said to Melanie, "Let me get this straight. I can live in this beautiful apartment with a roommate that I will hardly ever see, who possesses unlimited booze and have you as a neighbor for 250 dollars, plus utilities?"

"That's right," said Melanie, who was not only Miss Atlanta the year before, but was the reigning Miss Dogpatch USA (a beauty pageant held in the Ozark Mountains where the movie *Little Abner* was filmed). She drove a brand new Buick that had her name branded on the door, with a picture of Daisy Mae beside it. I swear to God!

"But Gary, there are some things you must know before you make a decision to move next door to me. Number one: I have a boyfriend. His name is Barry Buckelew, and you two would make quite a pair. Number two: I have a new roommate moving in next week who was Miss Florida USA the year I was Miss Atlanta. Her name is Stacy Evans and she is not only beautiful, but is fun . . . fun!"

"Where do I sign? When can I move in?"

"Hold on there a minute there, Cowboy," Melanie said. "First, you have to meet Peter to see if you guys are at least compatible. You should be, though, because his last roommate was also a young, wild man sort of like you named John King. John's the one who left that king-sized, round red velvet bed in what will be your bedroom."

"Wait a minute here. This guy isn't gay, is he?" I questioned.

"No, not in the least," assured Melanie. "As a matter of fact, I know that he does like to get away from Judy from time to time and kick up his heels with John and some of his buddies and girlfriends."

"Sounds like my kind of guy. When can I meet him?" I asked.

The following weekend, Melanie set up the interview. I say "interview" because that's what it felt like. I met the "prim and proper" Mr. Arthur P. "Peter" Hendricks for the first time on his turf.

I felt as though I was a potential employee, and Hendricks was hiring me. Peter dressed conservatively for a Saturday, with a sport coat and dress slacks. I think I had on jeans and a golf shirt. Peter questioned me about everything from my job to my personal habits, which were both fairly poor at that time in my life. I was changing jobs in real estate, and the market was not good. My finances were unstable, to say the least.

I posed serious questions for Peter like, "How do you feel about me drinking your liquor and bringing wild women over that may run through the apartment nekkid (spelling for naked, meaning you don't have clothes on, but you are up to something) from time to time—especially late at night?"

Peter informed me that it would be absolutely shameful if I had naked (only means you don't have clothes on) girls in the apartment and didn't give him fair warning, so that he could take Judy home. And, he added, it would be equally bad if he returned from Judy's to discover any lewd and crude transgressions taking place in the apartment in his absence.

Then Peter smiled with a sort of boyish grin and said, "Mr. Spillers, if you help keep the apartment clean and pay your part of the rent, I think we will get along famously. As a matter of fact, we need to go ahead and plan our first party to welcome you and your friends to Shadowood!"

I knew then that I was going to have a roommate I could identify with.

A week after I moved in, we celebrated our grand opening party with a roaring success and put a serious dent in Mr. Hendricks' liquor supply.

"Spillers," Peter said, "your friends are not only crazy, but they drink like fish!"

I remember worrying that Peter might not be able to replenish the liquor supply before time for another party the following week.

Peter assured me in his New York drawl, "Don't worry about the booze. I can get all we need. It's a piece of cake!" ("It's a piece of cake!" was a phrase I would hear Peter repeat a thousand times over the next couple of years.)

****

Peter and his friends got a good indication of what my friends and I enjoyed in drinks, music, and stories. Before the celebratory night was over, my friends Donnie Vance and his wife, Carolyn, brought Carolyn's father, Otis Lindsey, to the party. Otis was a hayseed farmer from Lenox, Georgia, who was also an accomplished pilot and crop duster. You could only imagine the stories he told that night out on the balcony of the apartment where he was holding court. The most hilarious stories were about his pot patch. Otis may have been from the country, but his two redneck sons turned him on to pot. As one of the area's best farmers, Otis grew a bumper crop of pot. Otis told us one day that he was working in his shop when he heard the crashing sounds of tree limbs breaking and this awful snorting and pawing.

"Hell, I didn't know whut in the world was a happening. I go outside, and just behind my shed was a big ole eight-point buck just a going crazy. This rascal was a jumpin' sideways, snortin' and pawin' at anythang that moved. He was a messed up, sho nuff! That joker had done got ta eatin' my pot plants and had done gone slap crazy!"

"What did you do, Otis?" his listeners wanted to know.

"Aw, I didn't do anythang. I figured that any creature that felt that good from eating all that pot would get horny and go on home and git him some, if he could find his way home!" said Otis, chuckling from his belly.

Then he continued, "It was 'bout a week later that I was in that same shed when I heard something a hittin' the side of the shed sounded sorta like a machine gun. It would go tat . . . tat . . . tat, tat, tat, tat . . . tat . . . tat. So I go outside and lo and behold, there was a huge drove of migrating starlings that covered my pot patch and was 'a feeding' on the seeds. They was 'a comin' out of that patch shooting way up in the air and 'a doin' lazy eights and shondells (aircraft stunts) and all types of aerial tricks. A pile of dead birds was damn near knee deep over by my shed. They wasn't able to pull out of their suicidal dives and had done slammed into the side of the shed, making that "tat, tat" sound. Damnest thang I ever seen!"

Peter was rolling in the floor. As a native New Yorker, he had never heard anything like this. For every party afterward, Peter wanted to know if Otis "was a coming?"

But Otis never came back.

When you are a farmer, in addition to being the mailman, the area crop duster, and local pot grower, you have very little time to attend a social outing—especially in Atlanta.

Being a quick learner, Otis had discovered that the big money was not in growing the weed, but in *transporting* it. Starting small, he worked his way up to hauling huge loads of pot out of South America. Then he got caught! Out on bail, he tried to make one last mega-run to cure his legal bills and was about to be caught again as his transport plane was being tailed by federal agents in smaller, faster planes.

Otis nosedived his aircraft into the ocean, causing his instant death.

****

Shadowood Apartments was without a doubt the most fun place I have ever lived. And this view about Shadowood is shared by many people. Barry Buckelew, Melanie's boyfriend, and I were constantly bumping into each other in different bars and ended up dating roommates and becoming best friends. Barry was dating Miss Dogpatch, and I got Miss Florida. It seemed fair to me at the time!

Other really close friends at Shadowood included Carole Reese, the property manager, and her husband, Terry Reese, a wildman from Lithonia, Georgia. Many of the Shadowood socialites had graduated from West Georgia College, except Barry, who eventually transferred to Auburn about the same time I matriculated at Troy.

The Shadowood gang shared the same impulses for good times. One Friday afternoon, I met a lady for drinks in the early afternoon at Ray's on the River, a nice restaurant and bar located on the Chattahoochee River across from Riverbend apartments. Faye was a beautiful woman in her mid-twenties who had been married for several years and, after her divorce, was either thoroughly confused or naive about sex and the single world. I was thinking she had bought into my idea of sex on the first date and the idea that women and men usually have their way with each other at all times of the day.

She said, "If all that bullshit is true, then let's go to your apartment and have sex."

"If you are waitin' on me, you are backing up."

We left the bar at Ray's on the River and cruised over to my place at Shadowood and had a great afternoon on the living room floor in front of the fireplace, and to tell you the truth, she wore me out! I had gotten up and slipped my pants and shirt on, and she was still stretched out on the blanket, butt nekkid. I heard a noise outside and saw Peter out the window, unloading his bags from a long trip. I looked back at Faye who had mixed a cocktail and was now sitting nekkid on one of the bar stools.

"Do you want to have some fun with my new roommate?"

"Sure, why not? I'm up for most anything," Faye said. So we put together a quick plan to surprise Peter.

Peter came barging through the door with his bags. I was sitting at one end of the bar with just my pants and shirt on, and at the other end of the bar was this beautiful, nekkid woman. Peter attempted to act cool, calm, and collected, but was 0 for 3 in that effort. I calmly asked him how his trip was, then nonchalantly introduced him to Faye who stood up and shook hands with him. Then, she politely asked if he would like a drink.

He was about to lose it. "Sss" . . . sure scotch and water would be g . . . good," he said. Baffled and confused, Peter began talking out loud about whatever he could think of (not unlike a lot of Yankees). He then made the excuse that he needed to call his girlfriend, Judy, who was on vacation in Miami.

Faye and I were still over at the bar, and Peter was across the room on the sofa, talking to Judy in Miami. As they were chatting away about different things, I whispered to Faye, "You said you wanted to have fun, so let's do it. I want you to go over and play with Peter while he is on the phone with his girlfriend."

Faye smiled. "I would love to!" She slowly strutted over to Peter, like a model on a runway. Then, she sat down next to him and started massaging him while he was talking on the phone to Judy. I thought his eyes were going to pop out of his head. It was a scream! Peter was trying to remain calm but when Faye touched the right spot, his voice would get real high and he would talk very fast. When she started to unzip his pants, Peter began talking faster and faster, "Jude, gotta . . . go . . . gotta go . . . I gotta . . . go!" and he slammed the phone down. I then went upstairs and left the two pleasure seekers alone in their bliss. I'm sure Judy wondered what happened, but I am also absolutely sure Peter didn't give a damn what she thought at that moment 1,000 miles away!

This Shadowood story is only the beginning . . . one time, we successfully shot a fireworks rocket from the bar through the dining room and out the sliding glass door. On the second attempt, it seems that we had a slight pre-flight miscalculation from NASA. The rocket flew through the living room, but took an unexpected right in the dining room and exploded in the corner of the dining room, setting fire to the carpet and the drapes! And never would we mention the party contest with a BB gun. The object of the game was to shoot out the playboy bunny's nipples on the centerfold hanging from the chandelier while shooting over the shoulder with only the assistance of a mirror—just like Annie Oakley in the Old West shows.

****

A couple of weeks later on a Friday afternoon, Peter came storming into the apartment and slung his bags in the middle of the floor, furious. He said he had to go back to the airport that night and get a plane to Miami to fire some guy the next day. He was pissed!

I interrupted his emotional purging. "Peter, do you know that Auburn is playing Miami in the Orange Bowl tomorrow night? It's going to be a great game! Why don't you get me a plane ticket and a hotel room, and I will accompany you to Miami to be your vice president of entertainment? We can take in the game after you've done your hatchet job."

Peter's mood changed immediately as he thought about the possibilities of seeing a good college football game, then going out on the town with me and some of my Auburn buddies who would be there.

"Sounds like a piece of cake, Spillers. Let's go!"

I quickly purchased tickets to the game and made reservations at the hotel where the Auburn team was staying. After we landed in Miami, we took a shuttle bus to the hotel. As we were getting off the bus, the first person we ran into was Barry Buckelew, my buddy from Atlanta. Barry, an Auburn graduate, had been working in Miami that week and already knew where all the parties and hot women would be.

The football game was terrible. Miami wasn't that good back then, and Auburn wasn't much better. I think Auburn won 7 to 0. A real thriller, huh? After the game, we ended up at a party where a lot of the coaches and ex-players were hanging out. I met Jake Scott, the former University of Georgia, All-American safety who was currently the All-Pro safety for the Miami Dolphins. Jake was visiting some old teammates who were coaching at Auburn. Also in the group was a former Auburn player who was then coaching at Georgia. We were all standing around, bullshitting, when one of the coaches asked Jake a question. "Jake, we understand that the Dolphins can run a man-to-man defense on one side of the ball and a zone on the other. Y'all can't actually do that, can you?"

I piped up, "Sure they can!" Then I explained in detail how they did it. Scott and other the two SEC coaches asked how I knew about the Dolphins' secret defense? I just shrugged like the cocky ex-jock I was at the time. "Shit, guys! We were running that defense seven to eight years ago when I played down at Troy State!"

I was incredulous that these two topflight SEC coaches were so clueless. But when I considered that our Troy State coach, Billy Atkins, coached and played alongside Hall of Famer Bill Walsh, it made sense that we would have an advantage in knowing cutting-edge coaching strategies that most college programs didn't have access to—even two SEC teams. In fact, Troy was running the multiple-receiver spread offense with no huddle when most SEC teams had never heard of it.

On the plane ride back, I thanked Peter for sponsoring such a fun weekend. He said, "Don't worry about it, Spillers. It was a piece of cake!"

****

Another bar and lounge that I frequented during the Shadowood days was "Gerald's," on Powers Ferry Road just north of Riverbend apartments. It was owned by the one and only Gerald Hensley, a unique character from the early Atlanta days. One day we were kidding around with Gerald and I said, "Gerald, I heard that you are queer. Is there any truth to that rumor?"

Gerald said, "That rumor has been blown out of proportion. The fact of the matter is that I will hold one in my mouth, but under no circumstances would I consider going up and down on it!"

****

The stories of Shadowood go on and on, but I would be remiss if I didn't tell this story involving Shelly Centers, the girl I dated the most during my Shadowood days. Shelly and I had met at Ray's on the River. We were smitten with each other from the git go. Shelly was a pretty woman with stunning, long red hair almost down to her ass and the personality to go with it. I cannot tell you how many fights I got into because of her wild ways. If she wasn't acting jealous and causing trouble, she was flirting with some other guy and causing a whole different set of problems. One such incident happened near the end of our relationship, and it was the reason we split for good.

Melanie disclosed to me one day that a couple of flight attendants had just moved into Shadowood, and one of them had gone to school with me at Troy State. She said her first name was Susan. Eager to find out who it was, I made a house call on the new neighbors. It turned out that not only did I know her, but we had dated for a while at Troy. Her name was Susan Gray, and she was a really neat lady. We spent that afternoon having a few libations and catching up on the previous three to four years, then ended up at my apartment, where I introduced her to Peter.

Peter immediately got the signal that I wanted to be alone, so he left to visit his girlfriend, Judy. Before leaving, Peter whispered that Shelly had called and wanted me to call her back. "No way!" I thought. Susan and I were having too much fun.

As Peter was leaving, the phone rang, and he ran out the door to avoid talking to Shelly, so I just let it ring. Fifteen minutes later, it rang again. I finally picked it up and got the ole "You're with somebody, aren't you?" Her speech was slurred, and her voice scaled from maniacal to depressed. "You are, aren't you?" It was obvious Shelly had been drinking. I told her I was keeping company with an old friend from school and winked at Susan who was sitting next to me.

After that conversation, the phone rang repeatedly. I finally took it off the hook. Things literally heated up with Susan and me as we stretched out in front of the fireplace.

Our clothes went flying like that passionate scene from the movie *Fatal Attraction*. However, close by was the maniacal Glenn Close character from the movie, now being played by Shelly, who had shown up outside and proceeded to bang on the door. I could hear her yelling, "Open this door you son of a bitch! If you don't open it, I'm going to kick it down!"

Thank God, the door was made of solid oak. Susan's eyes bulged with fright, and she commenced finding her clothes. I foresaw my much-anticipated rendezvous with Susan going up in smoke!

"Let's just ignore her, and she'll go away," I said. Susan's forehead wrinkled with uncertainty, but she nervously said, "Okay, I guess?"

It sounded like a frantic mob was outside, when suddenly, the living room window shattered and glass started flying. Shelly had thrown a rock through the window. She then reached in and unlocked the window latch, crawled through the front window, and attacked Susan in the living room. I got between them and pulled them apart, which was a lot harder to do with Shelly than Susan. Susan just wanted to grab her clothes and get the hell out of there.

About that time, Peter showed up, and I had a real mess on my hands: two mad-ass women, a pissed-off roommate, a badly scarred front door, and a missing front window.

I dragged Shelly up the stairs and basically locked her in my room until I could get Susan calmed down and out of there, with a promise that I would see her later.

Shelly wasn't going anywhere, so I resorted to threats that bounced off her like rubber bullets off steel. I tried to tell her that our relationship was over and she needed to go home. She would not budge. She was sitting in the middle of my bed and wasn't planning on going anywhere. So I said, "Fine. You can have this bed, but I am out of here."

She thought I was bluffing, but I wasn't. I left and went over to . . . you guessed it . . . Susan's, where we resumed our ill-timed bliss without the bother of flying glass!

The next morning, I headed back to my apartment and, to my surprise, there was no Shelly, but Peter had had an interesting night. It appeared that after I left, Shelly went looking for me, knocking on neighbors' doors and screaming my name all around the neighborhood. She even woke up Melanie in an attempt to find out which apartment Susan lived in.

Needless to say, I was not the most popular person at Shadowood that day. The carnage was abundant, and I had to repaint the front door and replace the front window of the apartment. Being a sought-after man can get expensive!

"God, that Shelly was something else, wasn't she?" Lindy said.

"Craziest damn woman I ever met!" I retorted. "That little altercation pretty much wrapped it up for us. Plus, a couple of weeks later, I met Cheryl, and all other women were put on the shelf for the time being.

"Shortly after the last Shelly incident, I began hanging out more in a bar just up Powers Ferry Road called the Chatterbox Lounge. I was pretty sure Shelly didn't know about it because I used to meet a former friend of hers there named Suzy White. As demonstrated before, Shelly was a little on the jealous side, and Suzy and I didn't want a debacle with Shelly, similar to the one that occurred with Susan at Shadowood.

Have you ever been to the Chatterbox, Lindy? Well, buckle up, you're going now!"

The Chatterbox during the mid '70s was the place to be for sports-minded guys and gals in the East Cobb area. Country music flowed, as did the whiskey and beer from attractive bartenders and wait staff who were second to none.

CHATTERBOX LOUNGE

Have you ever walked into a bar and immediately fallen in love with it? I came close the first time I walked into the Chatterbox Lounge. The bar had been recommended by a fellow "shark" Barry Buckelew. The Chatterbox had even been nicknamed "The Box" by former Georgia Tech football great Billy Williamson. (At least Billy told us he was great!) Williamson and Barry went way back, to the early '60s, when Billy played for Coach Bobby Dodd and the Georgia Tech Yellow Jackets, and Barry, as a kid, attended the Tech games with his uncle, Wilbur Bell.

One of Billy's teammates was Rufus Guthrie, an All-American guard and linebacker for Tech. In 1961, Rufus was the number one draft pick by the NFL Oakland Raiders' new owner, Al Davis. Rufus went to training camp that year and blew out his knee during the first week of practice. Tearing up a knee was almost always a career-ending injury back in the '60s, and so it was for Rufus. He returned to his native Marietta and began a successful career as a real estate developer and broker.

During the early '70s, Rufus teamed up with a guy named Lewis Ray, an Auburn man, in several real estate deals, and they eventually gained ownership of the Chatterbox Lounge in 1975. Lewis's family farm was part of the land that was purchased to build the intersection of I-75 at Windy Hill Road in Cobb County. During the Chatterbox days, the Rays' antebellum-style home still sat up on the hill where the Hyatt Hotel stands today.

Why did two successful real estate guys buy a bar? Who knows? But a bunch of other folks and I were sure glad they did! Initially, I think it was just to make money, but as time passed, it became clear that this was primarily a place where these guys could entertain their clients, bankers, and friends—including girlfriends. The Chatterbox stood out as one of the first true sports bars in Atlanta. Not only because it had good TVs, snacks, food, and game day parties, but also because of a roster of college and professional Hall of Fame athletes who regularly hung out there.

Representatives from Georgia Tech, Georgia, Auburn, and many other Atlantic Coast and Southeastern Conference colleges and pro teams loved the Chatterbox. Tom Lysiak and Eric Vail, members of the Atlanta Flames (Atlanta's former hockey team), were regulars, along with several of their teammates. They all had fun gambling on the bowling machine. Bunky Henry, an All-American field goal kicker from Georgia Tech who was later a PGA golf great, came by when he wasn't competing on the tour. Another regular was Billy Lothridge, Georgia Tech's famed quarterback, then color analyst for the Atlanta Falcons' radio broadcast team. One night after a rare Falcons' win, Lothridge was asked on air what he'd be doing that evening. "I'm going to Rufus Guthrie's Chatterbox Lounge out in Marietta. It will be hopping!" After Billy's endorsement, the place was packed that night.

The Chatterbox employed a very hospitable wait staff. The mainstay behind the bar was a good natured, no-nonsense lady named Pattie Casper. There was also "big-tittied Katie" (I never knew her last name) who bartended and waited tables as her day job, but these talents were minor to her skills in other places, according to a couple of my buddies. Of course, this was all just hearsay. Shelly Rosenbloom and her buddy Linda Louis were mainstays, giving great service in the bar. As a matter of fact, several of the waitresses were well capable of super-human feats inside the bar, as well as outside. This legendary service helped keep the customers coming back and loyal!

The Chatterbox music was a mix of rock and country tunes played on the jukebox. Live bands performed on the weekends, and if they didn't know "Blue Eyes Crying in the Rain" by Willie Nelson, there was no use in showing up. This song was the National Anthem of the Chatterbox Lounge.

Single people who frequented the Chatterbox had a hard time determining whether some of the married guys were with their girlfriends or their wives. One such problem surfaced one evening when my girlfriend, Cheryl, asked Billy Newton in front of his wife where Melinda (his girlfriend) was that night. Cheryl had thought Melinda was Billy's wife (not a girlfriend).

After that gaffe, the guys got together and decided that Wednesday nights would be girlfriend night, and Friday nights would be wife night. There would be no excuses or screw-ups! One wife showing up on girlfriend night would ruin everything! As far as I know, this system worked pretty good, as no public shootings by jealous spouses were reported.

****

One Saturday afternoon, I was supposed to meet the famous three T's—Tommy Arrington, Terry Reese, and Tommy Smith—for a late lunch at the Chatterbox, but I was running late. As I was about to enter the bar, the door flew open and out staggered the three T's, all drunk as monkeys on a merry go round! They were all arm in arm, swaying around the parking lot. I don't know how they were standing up.

"What in the hell have y'all gotten into?" I asked.

Terry, the most lucid of the three, said, "We just been gittin' shitfaced. Sandy's been takin' good care of us, so good Tommy done tipped her 100 dollars!"

"Holy shit, Tommy!" I said, "Did that include getting laid when she gets off? And, where did you get a hundred dollars in cash to tip a waitress?"

"It was easy. She took a check, and Pat the bartender cashed it for her."

"All I can say is you had better hope that check clears, 'cause if it doesn't Rufus is going to be after your ass!"

"I ain't worried," Tommy bravely stated. "I'll be back in 'Bumminham' by then! Hey, Spools (one of my nicknames), think you can take us over to Terry's? We're 'spose ta play tennis."

"Tennis?" I said. "There ain't a one of you that could hit a bull in the ass with a base fiddle! But I *will* take you home."

If you are wondering . . . yes, the check bounced! But after a life-threatening phone call from Rufus, which had something to do with physically removing a couple of key parts of his anatomy, Tommy made the check good.

I believe that some people just shouldn't drink, and Tommy Arrington was one of those people. Not that I should be left off that list, but Arrington just didn't have any brakes on his drinking truck. One night at the Chatterbox, we closed the place down, but not before getting a couple of beers to go.

In 1974, Powers Ferry Road was still a curvy two-lane road. We were driving my little red Mercedes coupe late that night and, as we were making our way home through the curves on Powers Ferry, the little red car skidded off the payment and hit a washed-out hole next to the pavement. The car flipped over and went rolling down a steep bank.

When the car stopped flipping, we were sitting there pinned against a huge tree, upside down, when I asked Tommy if he was okay.

"Well, just a few minutes ago I was having trouble getting my beer up to my mouth; now, it's pouring all in my face! Are we upside down?" Tommy asked, then added, "Do you think we should kick the windshield out to get out of here?"

"I don't think so. Why don't we just open the door?" I said. We then crawled to the top of the bank where we hitched a ride home. We called a wrecker the next morning.

Another memorable Chatterbox moment occurred at a Chatterbox Lounge customer appreciation party. Tommy and I were early on bitching at Rufus about all the strangers and people we had never seen who were getting better service than us. Rufus pulled me aside, and using his most courteous voice said, "Look you stupid motherfucker, these are my daytime customers who spend a lot more time and money in here than you and your broke-ass buddies. So shut up and get yourself a free beer!"

Daytime bar customers. What a novel idea!

Rufus and Lewis cooked a lavish feast of barbeque and baked beans. Bill Stose, Tommy, and I attended the party in Bill's company car. Bad mistake on Bill's part! We got into a baked-bean fight inside the car on the way home. Tommy volunteered to wash the beans off the windshield by peeing on it. That didn't work very well.

****

I don't know who came up with the idea of the Chatterbox Lounge Softball Team—I think it was Tommy Warner—but, whoever it was, he ought to have been taken out and shot. This was not a regular, slow-pitch team for middle-aged men, but a modified-pitch league team where the pitcher could not whip his arm around like a fast-pitch softball pitcher. The pitcher was only allowed to cock his arm back and throw. It was like hitting little league pitching at sixty-five to seventy miles per hour from forty-five feet. Another difference was that you could bunt and steal like in baseball, making it more of a speed game than a power game. Just the type of game a bunch of middle-aged white guys needed to compete in . . . ha!

It was a good type of game for young players. Not that our guys were that old, but we did have a few that, shall I say, were a little "long of tooth"! At the first practice, however, I was surprised at the level of talent we had on the team. Almost everyone had played either major college baseball or football. The roster was impressive. Billy Williamson played third base, and at shortstop was Billy Lothridge. At second base was a guy named Dell who had played minor league baseball. Rufus Guthrie held down first base. (Rufus wasn't that good, but he owned the team.) The pitcher was Tommy Warner, and in left field was Donnie Hampton. I played left center field, and at right center field was Spike Jones of the University of Georgia and NFL punting fame. In right field, and the self-appointed manager, was Don "Stumpy" Tomberlin (And, no, Stumpy did not have a peg leg, but he did only have one eye.) The catcher was Joe Chapman. Too bad we weren't playing football!

We started the season like "a house afire." We were beating everybody. I led the league in home runs. (You just have to take my word for it on that one. And that is exactly why as guys get older, they become better athletes than in their younger days. There are fewer people around to contradict their embellished stories and accomplishments!)

One day, as we were waiting for another game to end before we played, we noticed one of the teams playing was not only beating the other team, they were murdering them. On top of that, they were taunting and mouthing at the opposing players every chance they got.

The team was called P-Funk, and it was made up of all black, really fast players. They also knew they were good and flaunted their skills every chance they got at the expense of the opposing players. They wore funky, ragged-out uniforms. About half of the team painted their face one color and the other side of their face another color.

We didn't play P-Funk during the regular season because we were in different brackets. But if they won their bracket and we won ours, we would play them for the city championship. It happened! And guess where we were slated to play this seriously cocky, all-black team? In Grant Park, an all-black venue.

On the night of the championship game, a couple of our players suddenly were not available to play. We even had to take a fill-in guy named Paul along just to have enough players. When we got to Grant Park that night, no one was there. We just thought we were early and began to get loosened up for the game. Closer to game time, only one person was in the stands, and she was the date of our fill-in player. (Apparently, he didn't know beforehand where we were playing, or she would not have been there, sitting in the stands alone.)

We finished our warm-ups and were hanging around the dugout wondering where our opponents and their fans were. The umpire and his crew were there getting ready to go, but P-Funk was nowhere to be found. Stumpy, our manager, visited with the umpires and confirmed that if P-Funk did not show up in five minutes, the no-show would be a forfeit and the Chatterbox Lounge would be champs! In the next few minutes, nothing happened, and we were getting ready to go home with our forfeit, trophy in hand.

At the last minute, something strange began happening down the left field foul line. Over the left field wall comes P-Funk, jumping over the wall one at a time. Each player had a lighted sparkler in his hand. As each player cleared the fence, he joined in the other players in a snake dance down the third base foul line toward home plate, holding the brightly illuminated and popping sparklers crackling over their heads.

On this dark night, the sparklers illuminated the painted faces of the players and their crude, hand-painted gold numbers on their jerseys. Suddenly, the stands were filling up fast with P-Funk supporters. They had apparently been partying with the P-Funk players down behind the left field wall before the game. They went from having no fans in the stands to having more than 100 well-lubricated fans yelling obscenities and throwing liquor bottles on the field, and all this was before the game started!

As the P-Funk players reached the infield, the stands got rowdier. They continued to circle the bases in their snake dance style. We were just standing with our mouths open wondering what planet we had landed on. When they arrived at third base, they all threw their sparklers away and joined in a massive team huddle at third base, chanting with the stands, "P-Funk! P-Funk! P-Funk!" The players then placed two large cherry bombs close to third base and scattered away from the base as the cherry bombs exploded. BOOM! BOOM! The stands went crazy! It was GAME ON!

Stumpy got us all together before we took the field and said, "You guys know that we can get in trouble down here tonight, so go out and play hard and don't pay any attention to the extracurricular activities."

And play we did. We raced out to a 12-run lead and pretty much thought the game was over, but P-Funk didn't, nor did their fans. About midway through the game, they changed pitchers and they began to score. We couldn't hit the new pitcher. He kept striking us out. On one play, I was rounding third base, when the third baseman tried to trip me. When he did, I went after him, and just as I grabbed him to punch his lights out, we were separated by both teams. This really incensed the crowd, and it was now raining beer cans and liquor bottles again.

Stumpy flew out of the dugout, grabbed me by my jersey, and said, "Spillers, "THIS ain't Troy State! (referring to the small school I attended in Alabama) These motherfuckers will kill us! Now, straighten your ass up and don't cause any more problems!"

The rest of the night was one stressful situation after another until we finally reached the bottom of the seventh and final inning. The score was P-Funk 13, Chatterbox Lounge 12, with the Chatterbox Lounge coming to bat. The original 100 P-Funk fans had turned into about 200, and they were very vocal and very drunk. We managed to get a couple of runners to the second and third bases, so a base hit would win the game. But we had two outs.

Now, with the game on the line, Paul, the pickup player, was up to bat. (His girlfriend had been moved from the stands to the dugout for her safety.) Paul stepped back from the plate, surveyed the situation, and made probably the smartest decision he has ever made in his life. He got in the batter's box and struck out.

GAME OVER . . . P-Funk wins! The fans got crazier!

Paul later told one of our players he struck out on purpose, fearing the consequences of what would happen if he didn't.

We probably had the best team, but on that night, under those circumstances, the right team won instead of the best, and we avoided a lot of potential bloodshed!

"What a game! It's a wonder you didn't get in some serious trouble that night, and you probably would have if you had won," said Lindy.

"That's true, but did you notice what that road sign just said? St. Louis City Limit!" I said.

Gayle, the girlfriend of my buddy Phil Annie from Milledgeville, made good on her promise of putting us up for the night. Lindy and I treated Gayle to a festive dinner, and we took in some sightseeing before soon retiring to get an early start the next morning.

Hardly anyone visits St. Louis without taking in the majestic St. Louis Arch (at 630 feet in height, it is the tallest national monument in the United States). It was appropriately labeled for Lindy and me: "The Gateway to the West."

We slept well, anticipating our entry into Colorado and the Wild West the next day.

CHAPTER TWO

The next morning, Lindy and I headed straight west on I-70, the interstate that would take us through Missouri to Kansas City. It was there, at the point where the Kansas and Missouri Rivers converged, that the Lewis and Clark Expedition had set up camp in 1804.

Numerous billboard signs occupied every hilltop we came across on I-70. Though the drive through Missouri was hilly, you could still see patches of multicolored topography of oranges and reds of all hues, showing the hillside's last stand of colors about to be obliterated by winter's oncoming grip.

The drive through the state of Kansas was long and boring. Both sides of the highway were scattered with long gravel driveways. Barns and few trees made few appearances here and there. This scene must have repeated itself one million times before we made it through Kansas.

"I am still chuckling about the stories you told last night. Do you have any more?"

"Has a cat got a climbing gear?" I asked.

"To prepare you for the next tale, let me tell you about my hometown, Milledgeville, Georgia, the beautiful historic village by the lake. I have always been proud to say that I am from Milledgeville, even back in the days when Milledgeville's name was somewhat blighted because of its association with the Georgia State Sanitarium, a large mental institution. (The original name of this fine institution when it opened in 1842 was the State Lunatic, Idiot, and Epileptic Asylum. The name was changed in 1967 to Central State Hospital.) The facility began with one patient brought there from Macon, chained to the back of a mule-drawn wagon. At one time, Central State Hospital housed 12,000 patients. By the 1960s, it had become the largest mental health institution in the United States and was one of the largest employers in the state of Georgia. Today, it houses fewer than 500 patients and is virtually closed down.

"When I was in college, I considered Central State Hospital a plus for Milledgeville. At each school I attended, some of the guys would sooner or later brag about 'all the crazy mothers' from their hometown. So I would always say, 'I don't care how many crazies you have in your hometown. My hometown has 10,000 REGISTERED crazy people and more coming in every day!'

"Milledgeville is also unique for its rich antebellum history. It was the capital of Georgia during the Civil War. The governor of Georgia was arrested by General Sherman on the steps of the Governor's mansion, which later became home to the presidents of Georgia College and State University. During the Civil War, General Sherman spared the beautiful antebellum homes of Milledgeville by not torching them before he left. According to legend, this had something to do with one of the Milledgeville residents being a Mason, as was General Sherman. With two colleges, two huge lakes, the Oconee River running through it, and a rich antebellum history, it is easy to see why Milledgeville is a different, but special, small southern town.

"In Milledgeville, the hot spot for men in the '60s was the THE Milledgeville Pool Room."

THE MILLEDGEVILLE POOL ROOM

Back in the '60s, THE Milledgeville Pool Room was the epicenter of the Milledgeville sports culture. Local men would make an appearance at the pool room several times a week—for food and beverage, as well as gossiping about women, getting in a bet for the upcoming weekend of college and pro sports, or just gambling on the pinball machines or pool tables.

As you may have noticed, I did not mention women as being part of THE Milledgeville Pool Room. That is because I never saw a woman in the pool room from the time I was thirteen or fourteen in the early '60s until later years— maybe the '80s. Some liberal wench may have been the first to visit the place, obviously not having the proper respect for or lacking the sense to respect the pool room's hallowed tradition of "No Women Allowed". No respectable woman in Milledgeville would dare set foot in such a place in the '60s, and the men certainly appreciated their choice! Even the famous Pool Room chili dogs were delivered to the front door of the pool hall for loyal women customers who patiently waited out on the sidewalk for their culinary delicacies or had them brought home by husbands or sons.

In the early '60s, Mr. Alton Brookins owned THE Milledgeville Pool Room. Sargent Bill Tanner, an ex-marine drill sergeant, and his backup J.B. Hadden co-managed this fine establishment. THE Milledgeville Pool Room was one of three pool rooms in Milledgeville in the early '60s. But make no mistake, it was really the only pool room in Milledgeville!

Charlie Veach's Sports Palace, an inferior pool room with smaller commercial-style pool tables, was across the street under Belk's department store. Nonetheless, it was a haven for less-talented pool shooters and social misfits who were not comfortable in the classier Milledgeville Pool Room atmosphere.

Watt's Pool Room, the third pool room in Milledgeville, catered to the black demographic. Located on the "strip" alongside other shopping and entertainment areas on McIntosh Street, Watt's Pool Room was owned and operated with an iron fist by Red Herrin and his brother Watson.

Mr. Brookins and Mr. Tanner of THE Milledgeville Pool Room were good-humored men but, at the same time, put up with no nonsense from anybody. Both held especially tough restrictions on the use of the rotary dial telephone, located behind the bar. Use of the phone was a privilege *only* for regular customers, and even they were chastised if they stayed on the phone more than one or two minutes. The policing of the phone was not only for guys calling out, but also for guys getting calls from their wives or girlfriends. There was a pay phone situated in the corner by the front door, but it was only used when Mr. Brookins evicted some of the patrons from behind the bar for "over-the-limit" talking, or when a husband or boyfriend needed private time and was willing to pay for it.

Whenever the phone rang, Dickey Smith, pool shooter extraordinaire, would say, "I ain't here." Dickey's character could be summed up by the words of a country song: "Tell ole I ain't here, he'd better get on home."

If Dickey's wife wasn't on the phone pestering him to get home from the pool room, she was sitting out front in the car, blowing the horn. I don't think that marriage lasted, but THE Milledgeville Pool Room sure did!

THE Milledgeville Pool Room cooked and served the most exquisite chili dogs known to man. Like every other male in our unique little town, I must have eaten a thousand of them. These chili dogs became world renowned. An Atlanta TV station even tuned into the chili dog mania by creating a live, remote special on the legendary chili dogs. In their closing TV shot, they showed Mr. Brookins' son-in-law, J.B., stretched out on the front pool table, rubbing his big belly and saying, "Mmmm, them Milledgeville Pool Room chili dogs sho are good!" The late Lewis Grizzard wrote a book entitled *Chili Dawgs Always Bark at Night*. THE Milledgeville Pool Room chili dogs truly did bark at night!

Mr. Brookins and Mr. Tanner were always good about "holding" checks for the guys who shot pool on a regular basis; this cash flow tactic helped the gamblers get by until payday on Friday. Tanner and Brookins would simply hold the check until the agreed-upon day for deposit, then send it in to the bank. Sometimes, they would even extend the holding time for regular customers. Lex Sellers, better known as "Wex Wabbit," once had Mr. Brookins hold a check for a pack of cigarettes in the amount of twenty-five cents. Yep . . .

that's what a pack of cigarettes cost in 1967. Ironically, the check bounced! Mr. Brookins was not amused. He penalized "Wex" with a bounced check fee of five dollars, which screwed up the "Wabbit's" finances for several weeks!

On Saturday mornings every fall, the pool room was always swamped as the nine-ball games got started and outcomes of the local high school football games from the night before were analyzed. Last-minute bets on the college and pro football games were placed through a parlay (the practice of betting on several teams to win under one bet) or straight bets on individual teams with or against the assigned point spread.

Mr. Brookins partnered with "Jew Baby" Hawkins, the town bookie, who had a ticker tape machine set up at the back right side of the pool room that transmitted all the scores of the games going on that day. All the games and the point spreads were manually recorded in chalk on the blackboard by the morning of the game. On game day (a precursor to ESPN's "GameDay"), "Jew Baby" would delegate someone to record the scores in chalk on the boards as they were clicking off the ticker tape. One could "read 'em and weep" or rejoice as the scores were posted.

Saturday was also pool gambling day. The best shooters—Dickey Smith, Dodo Hollis, Wayne Samples, Robert Gillian, Dewey Brown, Joe Allen, Rembrandt Brooks, and Chester Gunby—along with a host of other professional billiard wannabes—always played on the front table. The front table was an open game for nine ball, meaning if you had the talent and money, you were in. The game would usually start out at a quarter on the odd balls and graduate to fifty cents, then a dollar or more on the three-, five-, seven- and nine-money balls before the day was done. If a player made one money ball per game he would break even, two would make it two dollars, three would make three dollars, and a run of the table would garner four bucks from each player. That was big money back then!

There were eight tables in the pool room. At the entrance, two snooker tables sat on the right for older guys and intellectuals, and six of the best full-size regulation pool tables you have ever shot pool on were located at end of the bar and lined up all the way to the back of the pool room. These were genuine Brunswick pool tables made in the approximate year of 1926, about the time that the Colonial Theater (the prior tenant of THE Milledgeville Pool Room building) opened its doors in Milledgeville with a Clark Gable movie. The entry lobby, with an original fan and tile floor with"COLONIAL" printed into the floor, is still there today.

Down the right side of the pool room were three pinball machines that paid in cash, if you were lucky enough to "hit" one of them. The machines noises blended into the crowd with constant dinging and steel ball popping noises. Some of the patrons of the pool room were addicted to gambling on these machines. The nickel coins that regularly dropped into these machines made their owner, "Duck" Harrington, a short, club-footed bookie, a very wealthy person.

The popping and dinging of the pinball machines, the aroma of the chili dogs cooking, the constant crack of the pool balls, the shouting of "rack" to the rack boys, the whirring of the ticker tape, characterized this busy, smoke-filled atmosphere. The voices of Chris Schenkel, Curt Gowdy, Keith Jackson, Bud Wilkinson, Dizzy Dean, and Pee Wee Reese (famous '60s TV sports personalities) set up and analyzed each game on the black-and-white TV sets of THE Milledgeville Pool Room. The sounds of the pool balls striking the keno board as gamblers pushed their luck and checked on their ongoing football bets between shots was a constant. These were the people, sights, and sounds that created many great and exciting Saturdays at THE Milledgeville Pool Room.

The survival of the fittest system in the pool room resembled a baseball minor league farm system. The best shooters commanded the first table, the next best group shot on the second table, and so on. Keno, a combination of pool and pinball, was reserved for many of the less-skilled pool players. Like football betting, it involved as much blind-ass luck as skill, kinda like football betting. Plus, the keno table was close to the ticker tape and the scoreboard.

Of course, all of these gambling activities were illegal, but the local law enforcement officials always looked the other way when it came to long-standing relationships and traditions around Milledgeville, especially when it was time to turn in their own bets.

A local wino we called Keno visited the pool hall regularly. I don't know where he got his nickname, because I never saw him play keno or even drink. He was just "different," but then we had a lot of strange people in Milledgeville during the '60s. Earl Johnson, another strange character, had done time at one of the rehab wards at Central State Hospital (a local mental institution).

One day, Earl shared a story from his days in the mental hospital. "I was walking down the hall minding my own business," he said, "and I believe I was drinking Aqua Velva (cheap aftershave lotion) that day . . . " Ugh. Like most guys would talk about the type of beer they had the night before, Earl prefaced his story with his preferred drink of the ward. I remember being so stunned and sickened to imagine that anyone would drink Aqua Velva, I didn't even hear the rest of his story. It took a pretty good man just to smell Aqua Velva without throwing up, much less drink it!

My favorite Milledgeville Pool Room character of all time was a one-eyed man named Bobby Daniels. Bobby was a good guy and was liked by everyone. When he missed a shot that hung up outside the pocket and didn't go in, he would yell, "Oh shit! I was robbed, raped, and fornicated, all in one shot!"

To unnerve his pool-shooting opponents, Bobby would remove his glass eye and put it on the edge of the pool table and then tell the eye, "You keep an eye on these motherfuckers up here while I go down to the other end of this table to shoot this shot!" I've been told that Bobby used this tactic while playing poker as well.

One Saturday during a busy time of day, Mr. Buster showed up to play pool. Mr. Buster was probably the oldest person to come in the pool room, and he wasn't a half bad pool shooter. Mr. Buster, Keno, and I ended up in a no stakes game just for the fun of it—except the loser had to pay for the game. About halfway through, Keno (knowing that Mr. Buster had just received his monthly Social Security check) asked if he could borrow five dollars. Mr. Buster replied, "I didn't hear you." So, Keno repeated the question. Again, Mr. Buster cupped his huge hand up to his ear and said, "There's too much noise in here; I can't hear you." After Keno's final, unsuccessful attempt to get Mr. Buster's attention, I decided to intervene. I got directly in front of Mr. Buster so he could read my lips and said, "I can hear Keno fine, and he says he wants to borrow five dollars." Mr. Buster said, "If you can hear him so good, then you loan the son of a bitch five dollars! I'm going to get a chili dog before y'all break me!"

THE Milledgeville Pool Room, like all gambling establishments, carried incredible highs and lows and great memories. It was a euphoric feeling to win a few dollars shooting pool or hitting on a parlay football bet, which put extra money in my pocket for the weekend. But like my former little league coach, Freddy Layton, once warned me, "Gambling winnings ain't good money! Because you usually end up blowing it and then not having enough to cover your losses when they come. And they will come. Remember, Son, the highs are never as high as the lows are low!"

Coach Layton was probably right, but the days I spent in THE Milledgeville Pool Room were some of the best in my young life. . . RACK!

"Hey that was a great man-story, but only if you are a man. I just can't believe you didn't allow women in the pool room," said Lindy.

"You had better believe it—all the women in Milledgeville did! Lindy, I know that you are a women's libber and you don't understand how it was in the South. This went on not only in THE Milledgeville Pool Room, but other places as well. No white pool shooters went to the Watt's Pool Room, and no black shooters came to either of the white pool rooms until the '70s or '80s. Men didn't go to women's places like hair salons, as they do today. And women didn't go to men's places. Well, except for one young visitor from Alabama who invaded another male bastion in Milledgeville that was just as hallowed as the pool room: Bobby Mercer's Barber Shop!"

THE TIGER IN THE BARBER SHOP

My good friend Tommy Arrington called one day to tell me he was dating a girl from Auburn University who was "a really nice girl"—someone he could really get serious about. My response was, "If she is all that nice, why in the hell is she going out with you?"

Tommy didn't appreciate my questioning his character, but he knew where I was coming from. He and I had shared the same girlfriend in college (not willingly, of course) and, after both of us had blown it with her, we became friends. A classic example of misery loves company, I guess. So Tommy was dating a "prima donna" from Auburn, and, guess what? She had a girlfriend Tommy thought I would like.

Tommy asked if I would like to meet him in Auburn the following weekend and go to dinner in Columbus, Georgia, with this girl, Margie, and him and his date. I said, "Okay, sounds good." Tommy then continued to make a BIG DEAL about how nice these girls were and how I would have to be on my best behavior all weekend.

Tommy continued, "Look, I know how you can be sometimes, and you just can't be a wild ass this weekend. You have got to be a complete gentleman and behave yourself on this date."

"Damn," I thought. "Tommy must really be smitten."

The game plan was for Tommy and me to get rooms at a hotel just outside of Auburn. The girls were to meet us at the hotel. We would take them to dinner in Columbus, and when we got back, they would go back to their apartment and we would stay at the hotel. How innocent is that? "Heck," I thought, "it might do me good to go out with a Christian girl every once in a while; it might help improve my attitude."

I was living in Milledgeville at the time, so on Friday I motored over to Auburn, checked into our hotel and relaxed until Tommy, the "convenient Christian" boy from Troy, showed up. Again, he was on my ass almost immediately about being a gentleman, and I assured him that I would be. Then, poking fun at Tommy's serious demeanor, I said, "But what if this woman is not what you think and she tries to attack me sexually? What am I to do?" Again, he sarcastically assured me that she was just a nice, small-town girl who had good morals, just like his new girlfriend.

When the girls showed up at the hotel, we met in the bar and had a couple of drinks. My date, Margie, was a really cute young lady with blonde hair and dimples, a pretty smile, and a great body, as was Tommy's date, Beth. They brought clothes for the evening with them and had planned to change clothes at the hotel, which I thought was sort of strange, but what did I know? When they asked if it was okay to change clothes in my room, I was really confused, but not so much that I refused.

After the girls were ready to go to dinner, we were to meet in my room and then leave from there. Margie was already dressed when I dropped by the room to find that Tommy and Beth hadn't shown up yet. This gave Margie and me some time to get to know each other and chat about school, the ways of the world, and what she would do when she graduated, which was about a year away. As we talked, she became warmer and closer, and before I knew what was happening, Margie was kissing me, which, of course, I did not resist.

I then remembered my pledge to Tommy and backed off suddenly, which seemed to surprise Margie. I told her I had promised Tommy that I would be a gentleman with her, and that was my intention. When I revealed this, it was like throwing gasoline on a fire. Apparently, the boyish rejection turned her on even more because, with a mischievous little smile, she said, "I love innocent defenseless men." I'm thinking, "God if she only knew . . . throw me in the briar patch!" My virtual innocence was saved for the moment, however, by Tommy and Beth knocking on the door.

We then piled into Tommy's car and headed to Columbus, about a forty-minute drive. On the way there, Margie was all over me. I tried to slow her down, but even with Tommy and Beth constantly "checking" on us, it didn't seem to matter. She was talking to Beth about sorority functions as she ran her hand inside my pants the first time! I didn't know what to do, so like a true southern boy, I asked Tommy something dumb like who was going to win the game that weekend, even though no one I knew was playing.

This was one hell of a fix. Here, I was trying to honor my friend's request to be a gentleman with a girl who was getting sexually aggressive in the back seat. Margie was ingeniously getting to know me better, while leaning forward in the car and discussing Greek life, football, movies, and whatever else came up. And believe me, something else was up in that back seat. Thank God Tommy had a big car with a large back seat.

When we arrived at the restaurant, I pulled Tommy aside and told him what was going on and who the aggressor really was. He admitted that he had noticed her boldness and was quite surprised—not only at Margie's aggressiveness, but that he was getting the same vibes from Beth. Tommy was beginning to wonder, too, about Beth's intentions and innocence.

"Do you think that this is a planned effort on both their parts to get away from the college scene and have a good time in the sack with a couple of out-of-town guys?" Tommy said.

"I don't know, Tom, but I sure hope to hell it is!" I replied.

As you can imagine, the rest of the evening went swimmingly well, as we finished dinner and headed back to Auburn for an interesting evening for both couples at the local hotel. Their apartments were never mentioned by either of the "innocent Christian girls."

****

After that weekend, I invited Margie over to Milledgeville. By this time, we both understood the game and didn't have the onus of Tommy and Beth as chaperones. Margie turned out to be a real fun-loving, free spirit who would damn near try anything once (twice or more if she really liked it). My kind of girl!

On the weekend I invited her over to Milledgeville, we went out on the town with some friends on Friday night, but came home early. I had to be in my real estate office early Saturday morning for an appointment. Margie agreed to meet me at the office around 11:30 a.m. to go to lunch, after I was finished with my appointment.

My real estate office was located in The Owen Building, owned by my good friend, Tony Owen, which was occupied with mostly accountants and lawyers as tenants. It also featured the "town barber shop" (Bobby Mercer's Barber Shop) as a tenant, located in the right front office space in the building. As you approached the building, the barber shop was on the right, and its glass door gave the barber and the customer in the first chair a view of anyone who entered the office building.

This barber shop was similar to any you would see in most small towns in the South. It had three barber chairs, but on this day, only two were occupied, and by the zaniest characters in the history of Milledgeville: Bobby Mercer and Howell "Rabbit" Horton. Bobby is a great American who publicizes his conservative beliefs and political stances. Rabbit, as his nickname implies, loves the women.

The crowd of locals that hung out at the barber shop was a cast of interesting characters. Nat Bacon, Lewis Peeler and James Cates were just a few of the "good ole boys" that had a good time on Saturday mornings telling lies, cracking jokes, and generally giving Bobby and Rabbit hell every chance they got. They filled the row of seats down the right side of the shop every Saturday morning.

I was just out of college and "wild as a buck" so, occasionally, I would have a good-looking girl visit my office. You know, for interviews and job applications and such. Every time a "good-lookin' little ole thang," as Rabbit would say, showed up at my office, Rabbit would be tipping down the hall, checking her out, whether he had a customer in his chair or not.

The Saturday morning visit from Margie is now part of the folklore of the Bobby Mercer Barber Shop.

My appointment finished early and Rabbit, who was also my mother's next-door neighbor, stuck his head in the office and wanted to know if I "was gittin' any?" I told him no, it had been pretty scarce out there, but I was keeping my eyes open, just in case. His response was always "You lying sumbitch, you getting all you can handle. I see these sweet young thangs coming down this hall. You ain't foolin' ole Rabbit!" With that, he went back to his customer waiting in the barber chair.

I had not mentioned to Rabbit that a certain Auburn Tiger (Margie) was coming by that morning, hoping she could somehow slip by the glass door without being noticed by his ever-present gaze. A few minutes later, Margie showed up in a short, low-cut summer dress in bright spring colors. Damn, she looked good. I was just sitting there admiring her, when Rabbit stepped into my view. He came sliding down the hall like the Kramer character in the Seinfeld show. This time, he was going so fast, he slid past the door, but he quickly recovered and popped his head back into my office.

"Well, well . . . who is this young dumpling? Spillers, I knew you'd been holding out on me. What's your name, dahlin'?" purred the sweet-talking Rabbit.

"Horton, get your ass out of here, and get back to your customers. As you can plainly see, I am busy with an interview," I said, laughing.

"Yeah, right," moaned Rabbit as he reluctantly shuffled back down the hall.

"Who was that? He was kind of funny," said Margie.

"Yeah," I said, "he's funny all right. He's my mother's next-door neighbor and a damn good one at that. He helps Mom all the time and I appreciate him, but sometimes he gets a little excited around 'good-lookin' dahlins.'"

Then, all of a sudden, an evil idea raced across my mind. "Hey, Margie do you want to give some old guys a heart attack, all in fun?" I asked.

She said, "Sure if it's not *too* wild."

"Okay," I said, "here's the deal. About right now, Rabbit is in the barber shop playing to his Saturday morning crowd and telling them all about coming over here and checking you out, so we are going to teach him a lesson. I want you to take your panties off!"

"Do what?" was the response from Margie.

"Here's what we are going to do. The barber shop is running about full capacity right now, the bullshit is flyin', and Rabbit is holding court for Nat Bacon and his buddies. I want you to take off your panties. Then, we are both going to walk into the barber shop through the glass door. I am going to stop and talk to Rabbit, next to his barber chair, and I want you to go over and sit directly in front of his barber's chair. Don't worry about a seat not being available. If you ask, somebody will move and move fast. Believe me. As I am talking to Rabbit, he is going to try to look up your dress, and when the time is right, I will wink. When I do this (wink), I want you to hike your leg up real high and cross it over, showing Rabbit and the boys EVERYTHING! The place will explode. Are you in?"

"Hell, yes, I'm in. Let's do it!"

Margie removed what little panties she had on and put them in her purse . . . it may have been her coin purse. We then went over to the barber shop, which, as expected, was packed. I stopped at Rabbit's chair, and Margie was offered a chair in front of Rabbit. So I started talking to Howell about everything from mom's garden to the weather, to the fish biting, and the new waitress at the Waffle House. Rabbit, for once, was not a good conversationalist. I had his ass in a bind. Sweat beads were popping out on his head and trickling down his face as he was trying to talk to me and, at the same time, trying to concentrate on cutting his customer's hair without cutting off his ears. Plus, he, his customer, and everybody else who had any kind of view, were trying to look up Margie's dress, without being noticed of course!

I then winked at Margie . . .

She responded with a high leg kick and crossed her leg, showing all! It was like a bomb went off in the barber shop. When Rabbit saw those legs cross, his electric razor dug into the back of his customer's head

"Aye . . . wow!" (sound of pain) the customer screamed, and then the whole barber shop began screaming with laughter. Rabbit didn't know what to do. For once in his life, he was snookered. I then stepped over and extended my arm to pretty little Margie, and we left a rollicking barber shop in our wake as we went to lunch around the corner at a place called the Pub.

About an hour or so later, Rabbit showed up at the Pub and semi-attacked me, grabbing and shaking me, but at the same time laughing so hard he could hardly speak.

He said, "That was the damnedest thing I've ever seen—but the funniest thing about the whole scene was what my customer said to me after y'all left. I was just trying to stop the bleeding when the old guy said, 'Don't worry about me, Son. After seeing what I just saw, I wouldn't have given a damn if you had cut it all off, ear included.'"

Margie and I never got back together after that wild weekend, but, wow! What a fun gal she was, even going out with a gentleman like me who, as always, was on his best behavior. Tommy would have been proud.

WAR EAGLE!

"Man, I thought I was wild in college, but I didn't hold a candle to Margie! She *was* a wild ass, wasn't she? Gary, those tales of yours sure brighten up some boring landscape. It's not that the Kansas scenery is ugly, it's just the same ole thing over and over again, VERY unlike your tales," Lindy commented.

If all the bullshit that came out of small-town barber shops was packaged as fertilizer, there would never be a shortage of it. I heard a tale once about another barber shop owned by my buddy Richard Burnet. It seems that Richard had a shop right on Hancock Street featuring a big picture window on the front that was a good viewing spot to check out the young ladies as they strolled by to visit the downtown restaurants and shops.

Richard had this one customer, Pete Baldwin, who was always commenting on the ladies as they walked by the big window when he was in the shop. He had gotten to the point where he was downright obnoxious about it, and Richard and his customers were getting tired of Pete's moronic antics.

On typical Saturday mornings when the shop was busy, Pete showed up and began his grading of the women as usual. "Man," he would say, "Look at the ass on that one" or "Look at the legs on that one . . . I'd like to have them wrapped around me" or "Wow! Look at those tits."

Every woman in town that passed this window got Pete's critical review until one morning a very attractive young lady approached the window, and Pete didn't say one word. But Richard did.

Richard ran over to the window and said, "Jesus! Look at those tits and that ass…"

He was interrupted rudely by Pete who loudly said, "Watch it buddy. That is MY daughter you are talking about."

"I know it is, Pete," said Richard, "but you have to understand that all of those women that you comment on when you come in here is somebody in this town's daughter too!"

So much for barber shops and Kansas boredom, we are about to get to Colorado.

"Westward Ho!" yelled Lindy.

CHAPTER THREE

"Yes I am a pirate, two hundred years too late

The cannons don't thunder, there's nothin' to plunder

I'm just an over-forty victim of fate

Arriving too late...arriving too late."

—Jimmy Buffett ("A Pirate Looks at Forty")

Certain milestones on a trip like this aren't necessarily earthshaking, but because of the time and place they happened, you remember them forever. Late in the afternoon, the western sky was poised, like an artist's painting. Beautiful hues of red and orange colors looked like they had been hand painted by the man himself . . . just for Lindy and me, as we motored by the Colorado state line on

I-70. As we trekked down the desolate interstate, traveling west, I looked in the rearview mirror and noticed a very strange vehicle coming up on us in the left lane. The vehicle was an even older car than the Green Pig, probably a 1960 Plymouth with the huge fins on the back. It resembled a sleek Caribbean pirate ship, appearing out of the misty fog to overtake us and pillage all our worldly goods. Piloting this craft was a hippie, with long hair and a tie-dyed headband wrapped around his head.

As he pulled up beside us, seemingly ready to cast out his gangplank, I said, "Lindy, get a load of this guy and his rig." We both looked and waved, and as we did, the hippie pulled out a huge joint he had been smoking, took a long drag off it, grinned at us, shot a peace sign, then "gunned" the big Plymouth's ample engine westward, disappearing into the red-splashed western sunset.

"Lindy, we just experienced THE COLORADO KID!" I exclaimed.

That scene was played out 35 years ago, but I still have the image of the "KID" sparing our lives and driving off into the western sky to rob, pillage, and plunder whatever stood in his path. I have this vision implanted firmly in my mind today as if it happened yesterday. It had to have been our official welcome to the great state of Colorado and the interesting things to come.

The first stop was Colorado Springs to visit Lindy's friends and area landmarks such as Pikes Peak and the U.S. Air Force Academy. Other than some impressive surrounding scenery, the rest of Colorado Springs was so-so, especially if you were looking for exciting things to do. At Pikes Peak, we took a photo and labeled it "The Pig Makes It to Colorado."

I found out the hard way at this stopover that Lindy was serious about the platonic commitment, even though we slept together. Not breaking the pledge really surprised me. I thought that she wanted and needed sex even more than I did. It's not like it would have been the first time for us. So much for being a "hunk!" I guess the only thing worse than being a "hunk" is being a "horny hunk."

Not a single flake of snow fell that day before Thanksgiving in Aspen and, for that reason, the residents and tourists were concerned that the whole ski season would be lost. From Colorado Springs, we had planned to take the back way into Aspen through Independence Pass, a small mountain pass a mere 12,000 feet in elevation.

By the time we got close to the pass, the Colorado Highway Patrol had closed it because of freezing temperatures and snowfall. I was pissed that we had to turn around and make a loop back toward Denver and back up to ole 1-70 West again. Lindy, on the other hand, felt relieved that we weren't going to attempt traversing the 12,000-foot narrow mountain pass in a rusty "bucket of bolts." The good thing was that it was finally snowing in Aspen. The other positive thing was that we were rerouted down I-70 and were able to take the opportunity to stop in Vail, Colorado, which literally sits atop I-70 West, just before Grand Junction, Colorado.

As total neophytes to Vail, we just parked the Pig close to Vail Village and went rambling around, ending up in a restaurant called Alfred Packer's, where you could get a man-sized steak. It seems that, back in the 1800s, Alfred Packer had been found guilty of committing cannibalism in the Colorado Mountains. The story on the menu made light of the conviction, claiming that the cannibalism charge was a survival issue, that ole Alfred was a good guy caught in a bad situation on a hunting trip that went bad. The story included a quote the judge made just before sentencing Packer: "Alfred Packer, you bastard! There were only seven 'demecrats' in the whole county, and you ate five of them! I sentence you to thirty days of hard labor!"

I have told that story a few hundred times over the last thirty-five years. After doing research for this book and checking historical records, I found that ole Alfie not only murdered the five men and ate them but also stole their wealth. He served more than twenty years in prison, being released in 1901 and later dying in 1907. Rest in peace, you cannibal bastard!

Another memorable thing happened when we were in Vail that day after we left Alfred Packer's restaurant. Lindy and I stopped in a coffee shop to get a couple of coffees to go. I remember taking out my roll of cash to pay for the drinks, and when I got back to the car, it was missing! All the cash I had to my name was missing. I bolted back to the restaurant, and when I burst through the doors, the cute little waitress who had waited on us asked, "You aren't missing anything, are you?" She then handed me all my cash intact.

When I told Lindy about it, she was livid. Instead of being thankful that everything worked out, she was mad at me for letting it happen in the first place.

"I can't believe that you were that damn careless with your money. Gary, you just don't respect money and what it can or cannot do for you. Please be more careful, or we are going to end up stranded out here in some God-forsaken place, and it's going to be your entire fault!" Lindy scorned.

This was the first of several tense moments between Lindy and me on this trip.

We again headed west on ole I-70 and shortly exited at the Glenwood Springs/Carbondale exit and then pushed south on Highway 82 toward ASPEN! We were both excited and awed at the same time, because the scenery between Glenwood Springs and Aspen is some of the most stunning in Colorado. The White River National Forest served as the background for the peaks and vistas as we traveled through the heavily forested valley that was traversed by the awesome Roaring Fork River. This historic river was the savior and slayer of many gold miners in the 1800s. The little stream could be harmless on one day and deadly on another, but treacherous or serene, it was beautiful as it snaked its way through the canyons from Glenwood Springs down to the magical mecca of Aspen!

When we finally arrived in Aspen on Thanksgiving Day, we were greeted by a light blanket of snow and our good friends, Jenna and her cousin Bryna McNeely.

Jenna and Bryna lived in a very nice little two-bedroom apartment only a few blocks from downtown Aspen.

Tommy had painted a glorious picture of the bars and the characters who frequented downtown Aspen. I couldn't wait to see for myself what this historical old mining town had to offer, as it was pleasing to both high-profile celebrities and snowbums alike.

The center of the universe in Aspen in the mid '70s was the Hotel Jerome Bar. At that time, it was an old ski bar. Later, the old hotel and bar was completely retrofitted, remodeled, and transformed to a rich man's playground as opposed to the old ski bar that it was at that time. And fun it was!

****

One of the first guys I met was Jim Whitaker, whom Tommy had befriended when he was there in the summer. Jim happened to be from Albany, Georgia. He'd come out to visit for a couple of weeks more than a year before and just didn't go home. Whit's family was well off and owned a huge John Deere Tractor dealership in Dawson, Georgia. I guess they sent him some of the peanut money to support his beer and drug habits out in Aspen.

Without a doubt, Jim was in second place to a fellow named Soda Pop Wilson as the lyingest character I have ever met or heard of. Nothing malicious, but as my old buddy Wayne Weaver used to say about Soda Pop Wilson, "He'd rather walk across the street and tell a lie, than stand on this side of the street and tell the truth."

Soda Pop "earned his wings" one day when a bunch of old farts were hanging around Dennard's Sinclair Service Station in Gordon, Georgia. Soda Pop came flyin' up in his pickup truck, slid to a halt, jumped out, and started pumping his own gas—a sign that meant he was definitely in some kind of a hurry! The old regulars sitting on old "Co-Cola" crates and worn-out cane chairs hollered at Soda Pop, "Hey, Soda Pop, slow down a little; come over here and tell us a lie before you leave."

Soda Pop replied, "I ain't got time to mess with you guys today. The courthouse over in Irwinton is on fire, and I'm headed over there to help put out the fire." With that, he hung up the gas pump hose and peeled off toward Irwinton. The old farts, not wanting to miss out on the action or helping out with the courthouse fire, all jumped in their trucks, burning rubber at high rates of speed toward Irwinton, about fifteen miles away.

When the gang of "firefighters" arrived in Irwinton, there was no fire at the courthouse. But there was Soda Pop Wilson, sitting next to the only red light in the county in his pickup truck. He was "just a grinnin'" when he addressed the group of arrivals from Gordon: "Do you gentlemen want to hear a lie now?"

Jim Whitaker was somewhat talented as a liar, but he couldn't hold a candle to Soda Pop Wilson.

****

The lack of snow was the main topic of talk around all the bars in town that year. So what do you do when you have a serious deficit of snow in the Colorado Mountains? You have a snow dance, of course. Newspapers and TV stations from Denver to New York City were notified of the big Snow Dance that would be held in Aspen on the Monday after Thanksgiving. All the major networks showed up to cover it, but so did all the characters in town who dressed in everything from clown costumes to firemen's uniforms. Everyone celebrated with a loud noisemaker of some type. The people chanted and snow danced, "Woo . . . woo . . . woo . . . . woo. . . snow-snow-snow-snow!" The whole town partied, and the whole nation watched.

Surprisingly, it began snowing that night but didn't accumulate much at all (made-for-TV snow, I guess). The next few days for us were a blur of partying and sightseeing. Aspen has an abundance of both. Whether it was taking in the babes on the deck at Little Nell's after the ski lifts closed or having one of the famous hamburgers at the Red Onion, Aspen had plenty to offer. My favorite was The Ajax Tavern, followed by The Crystal Palace.

The first day in Aspen, I met a waitress at the Hotel Jerome named Nicki Sneezik. I swear to you, that was her name. She was drop-dead gorgeous, a professional racquetball player, and on top of all that, a down to earth, good girl who liked to party with the best of them.

Nicki and I spent a lot of time together the next week or so until the Aspen part of the trip was over. Lindy and I continued further west. Nicki stayed in Aspen, but she later came to Atlanta to visit. During her trip, I introduced Nicki to a good friend named Tim Broom who was a former star football player for Georgia Tech with an ego the size of Stone Mountain—especially when there was a good-looking woman around. Tim's other hobby-sport was racquetball. After introducing Tim to Nicki, I told him she was a good racquetball player. Would he be kind enough to play a little racquetball with my friend while I was at work? After seeing how good-looking Nicki was, Tim agreed to play with her, but he wasn't "going to hold any thing back" just because she was a girl. Contrary to that initial declaration, he later confided to me that he would "go light on her" because she was my friend.

On the day of the match, I dropped Nicki off at the Riverbend Clubhouse where they were supposed to play. I told her I would be gone about an hour and a half and would try to get back and watch some of the match. My appointment didn't last long at all, so I hurried back to take in the match. When I arrived at the club, Nicki was sitting outside on the curb. When I asked her why she wasn't playing, she said that they were through. It seems that Nicki beat Tim 21 to 3 the first game and had him down 16 to zip in the second game. Apparently, he smashed his racquet and stomped out of the club without saying good-bye, kiss my ass, or anything.

Maybe I should have told Tim what he was up against Nah! Served him right! I'm just glad he took it easy on her!

Could Nicki be m'lady in waiting, if things went south between Cheryl and me?

****

Aspen is a place of incredible beauty, and the most picturesque area is called Maroon Bells, a huge snow-covered mountain that claimed the lives of some of the most rugged backcountry skiers in Aspen's history. A wintertime snow-covered lake sits at the bottom of the mountain, the ice glistening like diamonds, highlighting the textures and rigid knife edges of the mountain rock behind it. The lake makes summertime shots even more beautiful. Aspen Mountain and its famous ski slope, "Little Nell," is a must for all good skiers and "death valley" for all "wanna be" skiers who want to brag that they once slid on Little Nell and its slippery slopes.

We managed only a little skiing while we were there, because of the limited snow conditions. You may wonder how I knew how to ski, not having been around snow that much. In the early '70s, the Atlanta Ski Club leased a strip of land on the side of Vining's Mountain in Northwest Atlanta and cleared the trees on this strip of property to create a 1,500-foot artificial ski slope. An AstroTurf-type rug covered this ski slope with small polyethylene beads that, when sprinkled with water, gave an almost natural feel of skiing down a real slope. It felt more like skiing on ice instead of snow. But it served its purpose, and I learned to ski (i.e., start and stop, which is 90 percent of skiing) on that fun little slope.

The Vining's ski slope also featured a three-story lodge that housed an après ski bar on top, a retail ski shop in the middle, and offices on the bottom. For several years, the Atlanta Ski Club was the place to be in the fall and winter weekends. It especially attracted all the singles apartment dwellers in the area. This venue helped prepare many Georgia rednecks for the dangers of skiing out West and up North. We used to sit on the deck overlooking the slope and take bets on which redneck would take out the wooden fence at the bottom of the slope. Usually, their inept skiing skills would send them flying through the stopping area and crashing into the wooden fences that protected the other "skiers."

****

What we didn't miss out on every day in Aspen was drinking, usually starting at the Hotel Jerome and spreading to places that had the best happy hour deal all the way into the night. The Aspen Village carried a plethora of fancy and down to earth "good ole sports bars." One night we were in the Jerome with Jenna and Lindy when our buddy Whit showed up with information on another bar promoting a "killer" happy hour at the Red Onion.

So Whit and I struck out in search of the better deal. We later ran into Lindy and Jenna at the Ajax Tavern; they were in a high state of excitement, like two little school girls. Lindy could hardly contain herself. She grabbed my arm and said, "As soon as you left your seat at the Jerome, Jimmy Buffett came in and sat down next to me in the very chair you were sitting in. He was very nice and even bought us a beer."

"You didn't break the celebrity code, did you?" I inquired. (In Aspen they have an unwritten code that celebrities are to be treated like everyone else. Request maybe one autograph, but don't create any kind of a scene or you may get thrown out of the establishment or shot by a firing squad made up of bartenders who lose tips if the celebrity gets uncomfortable and leaves.)

"No," said Jenna, who having lived in Aspen for six months was now a veteran and kept Lindy's enthusiasm for Mr. Buffett in check.

After a couple of weeks in Aspen, it was time to move on further west. The night before we left, Jenna and Bryna cooked us a big dinner for a send-off party. Over several bottles of wine, we talked of Lake Tahoe, San Francisco, and the California coastal drive south and what fun we still had in front of us. It sounded so good to Jenna and Bryna that they decided to go with us to California.

Jenna had relatives in both San Francisco and Los Angeles and could be dropped off at either spot. We tried to talk Nicki into going, but she had a good job at the Jerome that she couldn't leave, especially with the snow season about to get under way. Whit couldn't go because he couldn't think of a good lie to tell his boss down at the airport baggage claim as to why he should leave just as the season was starting. Who would handle all that baggage? Maybe he needed to call Soda Pop.

The next morning, we loaded the Green Pig, which had been performing admirably on the trip. Several people commented during our stay in Aspen at how good a driver I was in the snow with that car and no snow experience. My response to any compliment was, "If you have never been on a South Georgia red clay road after a summer rainstorm, then you don't know what slick is!"

The next day, after saddling up the Green Pig, my "harem," Lindy, Jenna and Bryna, and I headed through Western Colorado toward our first major stop, which was Lake Tahoe, a trip that would cover several hundred miles. We headed west on I- 70 and then took Highway 50, close to Salina, Utah, just as night was falling. Highway 50 was a curvy, dangerous, two-lane road compared to the comfort of I-70.

Lindy had already shared with Jenna and Bryna some of my earlier stories. Later, they wanted to hear more, so as the Green Pig sliced and pawed its way through the Utah Mountains, I told the story of the incredible monster catfish, "Monster of the Deep Hole."

Monster of the Deep Hole

I, like you, have heard some tall tales about catching fish. Having been raised in the home of a local catfish-fishing legend, I can tell you that it takes an impressive fish story to even turn my head. My father, "Little Elbert" Spillers, was renowned around Milledgeville for his catfish-fishing expertise. He consistently landed fish when other guys weren't even getting bites. He held most of the informal records for large catfish caught on the Oconee River. But even Little Elbert's impressive records could not match the story you are about to hear as told to me by Jack Maddox, my long-time friend, confidant, and sidekick.

Jack Maddox is a wiry friend from my little league days. He has piercing eyes, a quick smile and even quicker wit, and very curly hair (hell, who am I kidding—it is kinky!). Jack has a presence about him that makes folks listen to his stories and laugh at his will.

We were sitting around the fire at our deer camp one night, sipping some Jack Daniel's, when the subject of catfish fishing came up. Some of the "monsters" my father had caught were topics of conversation. Jack, who was a good fisherman himself and admired my dad's work, said, "Well, Gary, I have a story to tell you about a catfish that I once caught that would shame anything that Little Elbert ever put in a boat."

This was hard for me to fathom, but I urged Jack to tell his story.

So he began, "It was a couple of years ago when you were off at school. Bill Massee and I kept hearing stories about this big catfish that no one could seem to land. The big fish's 'main most' feeding ground was the Deep Hole, a circular area in the Oconee River made by a huge bend in the river where an abundance of rock cliffs shot down into the river and above it as well."

I recalled the place in my mind.

Jack continued. "Nobody, and I mean nobody, could seem to land this huge maverick catfish. A couple of hardheaded, overmatched rednecks who would not let go of their lines were drug into the Deep Hole and never heard from again. Gary, even if your dad was still around, he would have a hard time matching up with this monster. The stories of carnage and destruction around the Deep Hole were rampant. So, Bill Massee and I got together and plotted an unconventional game plan to go after the Monster of the Deep Hole. Here is how we did it.

"I knew we had to get prepared in ways that we had never done before. This was serious business, and Bill and I didn't want to become another notch in the monster fish's massive fins. The first thing we did was go down to Cordele's farm supply and buy three miles of cross-stitched nylon plow line. From there, we went down to Floyd Couch's Body Shop and got ole' Floyd to "whoop" the top off of a '49 Ford and cut out a huge metal hook with his welding torch. Then, it was on to Joiner's Market, where we got Wiley Miller to fill up two five-gallon buckets with cow kidneys. We were then fully prepared with the proper bait and tackle to challenge the Monster of the Deep Hole.

"Upon arriving at the Deep Hole, word had gotten out that we were dead serious about catching the Monster, and the banks were lined with spectators. There were enough people there that day to fill the stands of the local baseball stadium. As we were trying to unload our equipment, we had to shove people out of the way so we could have room to work.

"The first thing I did was send Bill out into the woods to find a stout hickory nut tree that you couldn't reach around. The tree was located about a half a mile from the river. We went out and tied one end of the stitched plow line to it. The other end of the plow line was tied to the manufactured hook. We then made our way back down to the river where we hooked the cow kidneys onto the massive hook and threw the hook into the deep hole. I don't know how deep the Deep Hole really was, but I can tell you that a mile of that plow line disappeared into its the brown, swirling, gurgling, and bubbling waters.

"We then prepared a camp with a fire, sleeping bags, and chairs, as did most of the spectators. All the campfires flickered into the night and reflected off the waters of the Deep Hole, shining like Christmas lights in anticipation of the "great catfish" arriving. As dawn arrived, and morning light rays began to peek through the magnificent hardwoods and giant southern pines, nothing had happened. We and the crowd of spectators that had somewhat dwindled by then, were about to give up . . . when he STRUCK!

"When the Monster struck, it was as if a great tidal wave had hit the Oconee River. The Monster had never encountered a hook like this, and now he was irritated and pissed! When the slack finally gave out of the rope, the resulting pop and snap in the plow line against the hickory nut tree slung hickory nuts and several unwilling squirrels all the way down to Wilkinson County, several miles down the river! The waves got so high as a result of the fierce battle being waged against the Monster that several of the spectators were washed into the raging river, never to be heard from again.

"We played the big fish for two full days and used up all three miles of plow line. On the third day, we landed him. The big catfish resembled a small submarine, and the only way we could get him out of the water was for Cecil Townsend to bring his heavy-duty wrecker down to the Deep Hole and winch him out. The investment returns were immediate. There was enough scrap iron and exotic fish plugs stuck in the big fish's lips to pay for our expedition. We cut his head off with a timber saw, and sold the head to a guy over in Pendale for a two-car garage for his two Volkswagens."

"Damn, Jack!" I finally exclaimed, "That fish was *HUGE!* Just how big was this monster?"

"Well I don't rightly know," began Jack, "but we had to quarter the fish to get him loaded onto Bill's flatbed truck, just to get it out of the river swamp that day. Then, because of all the extra weight, Bill's truck got stuck, then ran hot and threw a fan belt."

"What did you do then?" I asked.

"It was no problem," Jack said. "I just went back and cut the asshole out of the fish, trimmed it up, then installed the asshole as a fan belt for the big truck and came on to the house. And you know, the last time I saw Bill he was still running that fish's asshole as his truck's fan belt."

Bill said, "It beat buying a new one, and best he could tell, the fish didn't need it anymore!"

"What a fish story! I'll bet ole Jack and Bill could have been elected to political office after that escapade." said Jenna.

"Gary, do you have any more fish stories?" asked Bryna.

"I certainly do." I replied. "But before we get into another story, have any of you guys noticed how light the desert landscape is? It's almost like daylight out there. The San Rafael Desert is huge, and we should be just about in the middle of it right now. We will be getting off I-70 pretty soon, and it will be like Lindy and I will have lost a longtime friend. We have mostly been on I-70 since we left St. Louis three weeks ago.

"Okay, since we are in the middle of a desert, it should be a good time to tell another fish story."

I call this one "The River Runs Deep."

THE RIVER RUNS DEEP

My father, Elbert Spillers, was a catfish fisherman ahead of his time. He held all the unofficial records for boating huge catfish along the stretch of the Oconee River from Lake Sinclair Dam all the way down to Dublin, Georgia, a good fifty miles. He caught fish when others didn't. When the fish were biting, no one could come close to the harvest that "Little Elbert" would bring to the house. Yes, he had a regular full-time job (albeit not much of one) at a mobile home manufacturing plant. Though he worked 9 to 5, he would usually head down to the river when he got off at 5:00 p.m. He shifted quickly from the job he hated to the job he loved!

My brother, Larry, and I would fetch the bait for Dad's trotlines and limb hooks after school. (Trotlines are heavy nylon lines, weighted down and stretched all the way across the river with smaller lines, with hooks tied to the large line about three feet apart. Limb hooks are long flowing nylon lines from three to ten feet long and are literally tied to limbs and branches that hang out over the river.) Bait-hunting preparations included scouring cow pastures for Catawba worms, catching bream and crappie for cut bait with cane fishing poles, or seining (a two-person fishnet pulled through the water) for live bait like frogs, crayfish, minnows, shad, or the ultimate powerhouse catfish live bait, baby eels.

Yep! You heard me right: baby eels. Baby eels are without a doubt the most deadly channel catfish bait ever known to man. None of the other catfish fishermen on the Oconee River even knew about baby eels or where or how to catch them. We knew all the details about catching bait. My brother, Larry, and I had a keen sense about how to operate and care for all of dad's fishing equipment. That's what this little story is about: borrowing my dad's fishing equipment.

My dad's fishing equipment, though not worth much monetarily, carried sacred value to him. He immersed himself in the ritual of fiddling with the different type of hooks, lines, weights, and baits that would work best in certain situations. He took pride in his fishing vehicle, a 1953 Plymouth that he absolutely loved. He had bought the rusty old car for twenty-five dollars from a guy who thought it had blown an engine. Luckily, one of my dad's fishing buddies diagnosed the problem as a fouled spark plug, which cost him only a few dollars to repair. After securing the vehicle, the first modification involved cutting out the trunk area to create more room to haul gear and to have a place to slide a small boat into, if needed. He also added boat racks on top to provide more storage room for other things like bait (alive or dead), trotlines, limb hooks, lead weights, poles, paddles, his ten-foot jon boat and his three-and-a-half horsepower Sears outboard motor. On an extended trip, we could store almost all of Elbert's fishing equipment into the old Plymouth at one time. I was never very fond of this vehicle because the doors would fly open when the car veered into a sharp curve or from any pressure on the doors from inside the vehicle.

During one of our after school bait-catching ventures, I was driving the old Plymouth along with our good friend

Steve Simcox, (a rather stout young man) who sat in the middle next to me and my brother, "riding shotgun" (the rider's side seat). We were headed up to the train trestle that crossed the Oconee River a couple of miles below Sinclair Dam. The driver had to negotiate a treacherous horseshoe bend curve in the old dirt road to get to the trestle. Of course, when we had no adult supervision, we always tried to "take" the curve as fast as we could, and this day was no different. Before driving into the curb, I revved up the old Plymouth's anemic little six-cylinder engine, popped the clutch, shifted up into second gear to pick up speed and attacked the curve with the vengeance of a NASCAR driver.

As we screamed into the vicious "dead man's curve," what hadn't been allowed for on this day was Steve's extra weight in the middle of the front seat. As the old Plymouth bit into the curve to the right, all the weight in the front seat (and Steve had a lot of it) went to the left against me, then against the driver's door. The door, under tremendous g-force pressure, flew open, and I fell out of the car! (And you may remember that I was driving.) As I was being ejected from the car, my foot got caught under the corner of the driver's seat. The car then dragged me about fifty feet before I could get my foot loose. In retrospect, if this had not happened, I would probably have been run over by a car that I was driving! After I got my foot loose, the car, with Larry and Steve still aboard, sans me, spun out into a row of plum bushes and stalled out. Tell that one to your local Allstate agent!

Larry and I over the years had grown to hate fishing chores. It had become a job that we didn't get paid for. Plus, we were made to go fishing almost every day from the time we were able to carry a bait bucket until we were old enough, big enough, and man enough to look the ole man in the eyes and say, "Dad, I ain't going today!" And then be able to back up this sudden assertiveness by defending ourselves against a serious ass-whipping.

Fishing kept us away from what we really loved—sports. Any sport, it didn't matter. We played them all, and quite well, I might add.

Ironically, all of our buddies thought Larry and I led the "Life of Riley" (a term from an old '50s TV show that depicted a soft life), but they didn't have to go fishing every day like we did. So, the kids around town constantly asked if they could go along with us. Dad would have none of that, because according to him, all these other kids ever wanted to do was play and have fun. Could you imagine anything as blatantly stupid as a kid wanting to have fun while fishing? What is the world coming to?

One day, two of my buddies, "Alert" Eddie Powell and Wayne Weaver and I were scheming up ways to make money when the idea of catching fish came up. I immediately squashed that idea because these guys didn't know "jack" about fishing, and I wasn't about to ask "Little Elbert" to use his fishing equipment.

Both Alert and Wayne thought this would be a lot of fun, and we might even get lucky with a prized catch to sell. After I thought it over, I agreed that it might indeed be fun, especially if the ole man wasn't along to boss me around. Hell, I would be the boss, and Alert and Wayne would take the place of my brother and me. This was sounding better and better.

The hard part was convincing Little Elbert to let us borrow his precious fishing equipment. So we approached him with the idea. He not only said no, but "HELL NO!"

I countered, "Dad, how do you really feel about this?" and received an unprintable outburst from him. I knew if I was going to get this deal done, I had to get my mother involved. Mom knew how Larry and I felt about having fishing shoved down our throats and was a little surprised that I would want to embark on a mission such as this. So, after Mom's guilt trip and coercion, plus my persistence, Elbert finally gave in—but not without telling me that if I lost one hook, he would "kick my ass from the river all the way home." I didn't believe he was serious, but he was!

The plan entailed fishing the area of the river just below Frank Lawrence's house where the river traversed through Mr. Carl Nelson's pasture. Mr. Lawrence, the Baldwin County Superintendent of Schools, had two sons by the names of Royce and Lawson who loved to fish with my dad from time to time. Their nicknames were "Patient," age 12, and "Pee Wee," age 10.

****

Mom once told me a funny story about those youngsters. Apparently, one Sunday afternoon, Mom and Dad had taken Patient and Pee Wee to the river for some leisurely sport fishing. She and Dad fished on one side of the sandbar, while Pee Wee and Patient were fishing on the other side, with a row of trees separating them. Mom went over to get some fresh bait from the boys. As she was walking up behind them, neither knew she was anywhere around. They were facing the river, watching their corks bob along in the swift waters. As she got nearer, Patient reached over and slapped Pee Wee on the leg and said, "Hey, Pee Wee, how 'bout giving me one of them god damn Pall Malls?" (Pall Malls were cheap, rough, unfiltered cigarettes.)

Mom said she had to bite her tongue to keep from laughing out loud. She just eased back to her side of the sandbar without them ever knowing she was there. She and Elbert had a good laugh over those educated, *proper* boys, smokin' and cussin' at such a young age. Ironically, or maybe not so ironically, Patient (Royce) died of throat cancer in his late forties, snuffing out a very prosperous and productive life way too soon. It seems he never gave up the Pall Malls.

****

So Dad granted us permission to use the fishing equipment. Our game plan was to go up to the dam and seine for eels on Friday night, then put out the trotlines and limb hooks on Saturday, bait up late Saturday afternoon just before dark, run (check on) the lines one time late Saturday night, harvest any early catches that night, and bait any empty hooks. Sunday morning, just after daylight, would be the big pay-off. Sounds simple enough so far, doesn't it? Even

Dad thought it was a good plan and said that we should be successful if we stuck to it.

Our first step was executed successfully as we went to the dam and caught all of the eels we would need for the weekend fishing expedition.

****

My brother and I had been using baby eels for catfish bait before anyone else on the river knew they existed. It started from catching small bait fish to use as cut bait with cane poles. Every once in a while, we would catch a young eel on the small hooks we used as bait. One thing was certain: If we caught a small eel and put it on a limb hook alive, catfish would appear the next morning 100 percent of the time. We used to believe that if we could find a reliable source of baby eels, we would be able to "tear some catfishes's asses out of the frame" on the Oconee river.

As fate would have it, we were seining for cut bait bream and crappie one day in the pool at the bottom of the floodgates of Sinclair Dam. The first problem we encountered was standing up in this slimy, concrete-based pool of water, which made seining much more difficult. As my old man used to say, "It was slicker than owl shit." The real problem was maintaining mobility in two- to three-foot deep water without busting our ass on the concrete. As we made our first sweep through the murky, green-stained water with the seine, we picked up a good amount of bream and crappie, plus an extraordinary surprise of hundreds of small baby eels. As we brought the seine out of the water, all of the eels escaped by sifting through the seine right back into the water. These eels were about the size of a small pencil three to five inches in length and were absolutely perfect for trotlines and limb hook bait. Eels were such good bait because of their tough skin and their durability that enabled them to stay alive for days wiggling away in the water until a hungry fish came along and struck. The opportunity (or the problem) we now had was how to harvest the slippery critters.

The first thing we had to figure out was how in the hell were we going to stand up while seining for them. We solved the problem by wearing metal baseball cleats. Those slick walls were reduced to mere child's play when we put on our baseball cleats before seining. Next was installing a screen wire to the seines.

After those adjustments, as the seine came out of the water, we had a much better chance at getting the eels into a waiting bucket of water for transport down to the river. The screen wire worked okay, but it wasn't until late one day, just before dark, when we discovered that the eels came out of the water at night and climbed up onto the flood gate walls where streams of water from the dam flowed over them. After we found out about the eels coming out at night, we just used screen wire nets to harvest them from the walls.

After all this research and development, a major problem still existed: transporting the eels in five-gallon buckets of water. The eels lacked oxygen in the water buckets, and the water level was much too high. Plus, we had to tote the full buckets of water up the rocky steep banks of Sinclair

Dam, a distance of a quarter mile almost straight up to a parking area. (Are you getting a picture of why my brother and I became great athletes? More on this later.)

We finally got a break one day. We handled the eels by immersing them in sand; the grit in the sand allowed us to hold them still long enough to bait them with the hook. After baiting up with eels one night, we had several of them left over, so we just left them to die in the wet sand. But, guess what? When we came back the next day, all of the eels were alive and well in the wet sand.

What we learned that day was huge! Instead of hauling the five-gallon buckets of water around and still losing half of our live bait to suffocation, we just put wet sand in the bottom of big No. 2 wash tubs, and the eels did just fine.

****

Wayne, Alert Eddie, and I had the bait ready to go, so on Saturday morning, we headed down to the river past Mr. Lawrence's house and down through Mr. Carl Nelson's pasture to our improvised boat landing. We parked the Plymouth on the edge of the riverbank, far enough from the river so that any normal rising river water would not get to it.

We unloaded the little jon boat, then attached the outboard motor, making sure it was full of fuel and that all of the trotlines and limb hooks were accounted for and ready to go. I was beginning to believe that Alert and Wayne were not too bad as fishermen until we got into the boat. It was a major struggle for the next two days just to keep them in the boat, much less on task. Every question I asked of Alert was answered with a . . . "Huh?" and Wayne wasn't much better. Actually, they did okay the first day, because they did exactly what I told them to do. Hell, I liked being the boss!

Wayne confided in me that day that he had had some creative experience catching bait while fishing at the same time. It seems that Wayne went fishing by himself one morning and ran out of his short supply of worms. Looking around for some type of bait, he discovered a cottonmouth moccasin with a frog in his mouth. Knowing that the snake couldn't bite him with the frog in his mouth, he grabbed him behind the head, took the frog and put it in his bait bucket. Now the dilemma was how to release the snake without getting bit. So he grabbed his bottle of Jack Daniel's Black from his tackle box and poured a little of the sweet liquid into the snake's mouth. The snake's eyes rolled back, and he went limp. Wayne then released the snake back into the river without incident and continued fishing, using the frog. A little later Wayne felt a nudge on his foot. He looked down, and there was the same snake with TWO frogs in his mouth!

We were able to get out four trotlines with about fifty hooks on each one. The selected locations were all perfect places in the river just under shoals and big bends. Most harbored deep water on one side and sandbars or shallow water on the other. We also got out about twenty-five limb hooks in excellent spots that I knew would yield some big "cats." It took us several hours to get the hooks out and by the time we were finished, it was time to start baiting up. The baiting-up process took about two hours, and we finished just before dark. I was confident that everything had been done properly, and we would be loaded with fish by the next morning just after daylight. The one thing that I hadn't checked on was the weather forecast.

The initial plan was to camp out at the river and check the hooks around 11:00 p.m. and be there at daylight to harvest our yield. The best-laid plans are made to be broken aren't they?

Alert, though not the sharpest tool in the shed, was a good-looking guy and very successful with the ladies. He had found out about a little social function involving a few ladies of questionable character that was going down that night, and we surely did not want to miss out. So we decided to go party a while, then go down and check the hooks later. As we were doing all this high-level planning, rain was beginning to fall, heavy rain!

The game plan was now altered to meet at Wayne's house and head to the river at 11:00 p.m. So around 12:00 a.m. we headed out, still in a pouring rain that had been going on heavily for several hours. Driving in that rain in the old Plymouth was a challenge even on good roads, but when we hit the pasture road, I couldn't see a thing. We decided to shut it down in the pasture road and wait out the storm. It rained all night and any plans of "running" the hooks at midnight were no longer a reality. We would sleep in the car and wait for daylight.

Daylight came the next morning with clear skies, but instead of being in the pasture road, we were parked out in the middle of the pasture without a road in sight. I told you I couldn't see! We got the old Plymouth fired up and headed for the boat ramp.

Before we reached the river, we had to cross Murder Creek, which had been a trickle of a stream the day before, but was now much higher than usual after the heavy rains. It was a bit of a struggle to get the old Plymouth through. But we did, and as soon as we reached the river, I knew three things. Number one, the current of the river was flowing even with the river banks, which meant that that Sinclair Dam had opened a couple, or more, of its floodgates and the river was rising. Number two, the likelihood of retrieving my dad's trotlines and limb hooks was almost zero. And number three, with Alert and Wayne as co-captains, we would be lucky if we didn't drown, much less find many of the hooks. Good guys they were. River rats, like my brother and me, they were not.

We probably should have turned around and sought higher ground immediately, but we didn't. I thought, being the seasoned riverboat captain that I most certainly was, that we might have time to save most of the hooks. Plus, when the river is rising, the fish go into a feeding frenzy and hit everything in the water. I was right about that. Almost every hook we could find had a fish on it. The problem was we couldn't get to many hooks. The little three-and-a-half horse-powered Sears outboard motor was no match for the swift, churning reddish-brown waters of the Oconee River. Fueled by the onslaught of overnight storms that had engulfed and covered all the trotlines and most of the limb hooks, the raging Oconee River was stretching its deadly brown tentacles and looking for more victims. The way I saw it, we were next!

After quickly assessing our situation as "Code Red," we headed back to the quickly disappearing boat landing to load the boat, the motor, and what fishing tackle we had left.

The equipment loading was the last thing that went smoothly that day. As soon as that was accomplished, we jumped in the old Plymouth and hit the ignition . . . nothing! We tried everything, but couldn't get it to turn over or even think about cranking. The river was rising. We knew we had to do something, and do it fast, when Wayne came up with a wise idea for a change. When we had met at his house the night before, his uncle was visiting for the weekend and was in his new F-100 Ford pickup truck. He would surely come down to the river and help us out. The only problem was that we would have to run at least four or five miles through the rain-soaked pastures to get to Wayne's house. We just had to hope his uncle would still be there. After thinking about it a couple of seconds, I said, "Let's go." We left Alert with the equipment and hauled ass, running toward Wayne's house.

At the conclusion of our mini-marathon through the pastures, creeks, and briar patches, we arrived at Wayne's house to find no one there. But his uncle had left his new truck sitting in the driveway, with the keys in the ignition! After a couple of minutes of soul-searching, we made another "wise" decision. Surely, Wayne's uncle wouldn't mind if we borrowed his new truck? We quickly left a note for him, got in the truck, and sped back to Murder Creek.

The water was even deeper when we returned to Murder Creek, but we got through it to the boat ramp area, where we tried to jump off the car. Nothing again! The new plan was to use the truck to tow the Plymouth up to higher ground. So, we hurriedly got the Plymouth chained to the back of the truck and almost immediately got the truck stuck down to the axles in the soft, water-soaked ground. Now we really were in a bind! Two vehicles stuck, and the river was rising. This was getting serious. If we lost both those vehicles, the three of us might as well get into that boat and head for Savannah or someplace really remote.

Then, an idea hit me. I had stopped by Mr. Lawrence's house a couple of weeks before and had seen an old Willis jeep under one of his sheds. If that jeep was running, it would be exactly what we need to get these vehicles out.

Mr. Lawrence's house was only about a mile or so away—a mere pittance to someone who had just run five miles. So, off we went to the Lawrences' house. There, we found only Mrs. Martha Lawrence at home (who, by the way, was my favorite substitute school teacher of all time). Mrs. Lawrence told us that we were welcome to use the jeep, but she didn't know if it would even crank. It did, and we hurried back to save the two vehicles from the rising river!

When we got to Murder Creek just before the boat landing, the water level was even higher than before but, hey, we were in a military jeep, just like the one used to drive General Patton around during the war. This little ole creek ain't shit! Famous last words! We drowned the jeep's engine out in the middle of Murder Creek. And the river continued to rise!

Let's recalculate. We have the ole Plymouth that won't crank, chained to the stuck pickup truck, and we now have the superintendent of school's jeep drowned out in a rising creek bed. The river was rising and we were sunk!

But not quite! As I looked out over the horizon, I thought I saw Mr. Carl Nelson coming across the pasture in his beautiful, blue four-wheel drive truck. Then it disappeared! Was it a mirage? No, there it is again; now it's gone.

From the long distance across the pastures, Mr. Carl's truck was going down, into and up out of gulleys. It appeared as though the truck was disappearing, but sure enough it really was Mr. Nelson, so we sprinted (yet again) across the pasture to flag him down and hurriedly explain the dire situation we were in.

Mr. Carl wasted no time. First, he crashed into Murder Creek and pulled the Willis jeep to safety. Then, he went back and pulled Wayne's uncle's new, red mud-caked truck to high ground and out of harm's way. But when it was time to return to get the old Plymouth, it was too late! The water in Murder Creek had already risen to a level where it would be to unsafe to chance going back in for the car.

Faced with the prospect of losing not only my dad's fishing car, but all of his equipment, we waded back into the boat ramp area to see what we could save. The water was already about halfway over the tires of the old Plymouth. We unloaded the boat from the vehicle and used it like a packhorse. It was filled with all the fishing equipment, the motor, and what hooks we were able to rescue, as well as about forty to fifty pounds of catfish from the morning harvest.

The totally exhausted three stooges of the river were paddling out of what used to be the boat ramp area toward the bank when the worst-case scenario played itself out.

There, standing on a fast-disappearing pasture knoll was my dad, Wayne's dad, and Wayne's slightly irritated uncle (who wasn't particularly happy with our decision to steal his truck). It was a bad day at Black Rock! (The mythical western town where nothing good ever happens had stretched its boundaries to the banks of the Oconee River.)

My dad immediately started threatening me and picked up a limb to hit me with, but then thought better of it. Wayne was getting his ass chewed out, too. And Alert was just thinking . . . "Huh?"

After all the tempers were somewhat cooled, my old man decided that, instead of killing us, he would give us the "opportunity" for redemption by having us clean 300 pounds of stored catfish—for no pay.

Things settled back to normal, as well as could be expected.

As our virtual motorcade of vehicles was leaving the river, I took one last look out across the rising, swirling, brown waters, and all I could see of the old Plymouth was the boat racks on top of the car . . . and a river running through them!

CHAPTER FOUR

As I finished the last story, the ladies were quiet for a moment. Then they all confessed that, after that exhaustive tale, they needed a break! We were just approaching a town named Delta, Utah, where they could possibly get some relief. I swear to God, you could replace the cars and trucks with horses and buggies in Delta, and you would have been on a western cowboy town movie set. As we pulled into town, the only thing open was the saloon. So we parked the car and went in.

The only inhabitants in the bar were involved in a blackjack game with the bartender who was about 6 feet tall and 230 pounds and just happened to be a woman. She was playing with a couple of rough-looking cowboys. As the ladies headed to the restroom, I asked if I could join the game.

"If you got the cash for five dollars per hand, you're in," was the bartender's response.

I got in and won the first five hands. This did not set too well with the bartender or the cowboys. On the sixth hand, it was my time to deal. About this time, the girls were getting restless to get back on the road, and my new friends were not happy with me either. I dealt the cards down and didn't look at mine until everyone had placed their bets. I then looked at my hand, and it was a pure blackjack!

I looked at the NFL–sized bartender lady and the two unhappy cowboys, folded my hand, took my cash, and hit the door. I still believe if I had blackjacked on those guys with me dealing, there would have been some serious medical consequences. And serious medical consequences we didn't need. All we needed was to get back on Highway 50 and head west across the Great Basin and the Sevier Desert, then over the awesome Confusion Range of Utah into Nevada.

Even though I had "copped" a quick seventy-five dollars, Lindy wasn't at all happy because she didn't believe in gambling and, according to her, I could have gotten involved in a serious altercation with those cowboys. Lindy's whole demeanor seemed to change, and I didn't like what I was hearing. It was probably the lack of sex she was experiencing, or sour grapes that she hadn't taken me up on my generous offers from time to time. Who knows and who cares? Come on, California!

Swapping out drivers was easy with so many bored souls. As we switched drivers and covered ground, the ladies wanted to know about my college experiences, so I relayed "Three Schools Are Better Than One."

THREE SCHOOLS ARE BETTER THAN ONE

I was fortunate enough to attend three fine, albeit small, southern universities. (They were colleges then.) During the mid to late '60s, it seemed that every small school that was a college wanted to change its status to become a university. I never saw any material evidence that being a university made any difference in any of the schools, one way or the other. I guess it boiled down to the fact that "University" just sounded more important and prestigious. It certainly didn't change the student profile that was attracted to the small college.

Each of the three institutions I attended—Austin Peay State University (APSU), Georgia College, and Troy State University— had either just changed its status to university or was in the process of changing in the near future.

If there was ever a school that needed a name change, that would have been Austin Peay (pronounced Pee), named after a famous past governor. All buildings on campus were also named after past Tennessee governors. And I swear to God, the battle cry for the sports teams was "Let's Go Pee," complete with pee pots brought to the game by fans to cheer the Governors on. Yep, you heard right: "Let's Go Pee!" . . . "Go Governors!" Kinda grows on you, doesn't it?

As a matter of fact, in early 1967, there was a strong movement in the Tennessee State Legislature to change the name of Austin Peay State College to North Tennessee State University, pretty nifty I thought. This nifty idea was voted out in a landslide by the Austin Peay Alumni Association backers. My guess is that anyone who had had to yell "Let's Go Pee" and wave a pee pot during their college years would want to wish it on everyone who followed in his or her footsteps at ole APSC . . . or is it APSU? I get confused.

I left Milledgeville, Georgia, in the late summer of 1966 on a Greyhound bus with my good friend Wayne Weaver. Both of us had received football scholarships to play for the Austin Peay State University Governors.

The bus trip was supposed to be a six- to eight-hour ride at the most. It took us twenty-four hours! We ran into a girl on the bus that we went to high school with who had an apartment in Atlanta. Need I say more? That trip should have told me something about my upcoming college career. Ronnie Simpson, another guy from Milledgeville who was already in Clarksville, went to the bus station in Clarksville, Tennessee, five or six different times to pick us up, but to no avail.

Even though Clarksville and Milledgeville were both college towns, they were very different. For one thing, Milledgeville didn't have a major army base ten miles away with a training camp for the U.S. Army's 101st Airborne Division as did Clarksville. Also, my college years were during the height of the Vietnam War. There used to be a saying that the hand-to-hand combat that they teach you in the army only prepares you to go downtown on Saturday night and get your ass kicked. It was true. The soldiers from Fort Campbell would get "liquored up" and come to Clarksville on Saturday night to show off their newly learned pugilistic skills, and we would whip their asses and send them back to the base singing "Sonny Boy".

Fighting soldiers was about the only recreation there was in Clarksville, that is, until the students showed up on campus to begin classes. But when the ladies arrived, we were terribly disappointed. The guys from Georgia thought this was the ugliest bunch of women on one campus, at one time— ever. Austin Peay girls weren't *that* bad, but they sure as hell had a hard time fielding a homecoming court without recruiting talent from the local Waffle House. Okay, it really wasn't hopeless, but being from a college town with an all-women's college, let's just say that I had to dial my cull factor back a notch or two.

Although the girls weren't that great, some of the guys I met at Austin Peay are still buddies of mine today: Wayne Weaver, Ronnie Simpson, Tony Stubbs, Tony Layfield, Jimmy Hardie, and David Dukes, to name a few. My favorite character at Austin Peay was a baseball player from Knoxville, Tennessee, named Dwight Smith. Dwight was in love with baseball. He lived it and breathed it. After a couple of beers, he used to say, "My name is Dwight D from Knoxville, Tennessee" and break down like a catcher, demonstrating how to properly block home plate, no matter where we were at the time.

One of the funniest things I have ever seen in intramural, or any type of sports, happened to Dwight and Larry Jones, a teammate of his during an intramural basketball game. Dwight had taken the ball out of bounds under the basket and spotted another teammate running free down the court. With Dwight's cannon of an arm, he drew back to throw the ball the entire length of the court, but nobody told Larry, the point guard, who usually received an underhanded toss as an inbounds pass. As Larry turned to receive the soft toss, he caught Dwight's ninety-mile-per-hour missile—square in the face. The first thing to hit the floor was the back of Larry's head (and Larry was a big ole boy). After the smelling salts took effect and Larry regained his faculties, he began screaming offensive expletives at Dwight and chasing him around the gym, out the door, and across the campus. That officially ended the basketball game.

As far as college football is concerned, ole APSU wasn't much, but it's where I got started, so I will always have a soft spot in my heart for it.

One day in class, we were talking about how bad our Austin Peay football team was when my professor told us about his hometown high school team—the worst high school team ever. It seems that in the professor's senior year, they lost all of their regular season games once again. Then the people of the little town devised a scheme to ensure that they would still win at least one game that year. So they divided the team into two teams and scheduled an intersquad game. After playing each other until it got dark, no one had scored, so the townspeople said "to hell with it" and accepted their fate as the worst high school. EVER!

I will always remember my first college football practice. We were to practice twice a day for the first week, then only one longer practice per day until the fall season started. That first practice was brutal. The coaches wanted to see early who the men were and who would be shown the door. The first practice started at 9:00 a.m., and for North Tennessee, the weather was extremely hot! I wanted to make an impression early, and I did with several vicious hits, not only delivered but received. They ran us a lot and put the new guys through several agility drills. When the final whistle was blown to end the morning practice, my knees were a little rubbery, and my head was spinning as we left the field. This was not high school football!

I remember going to lunch that day and eating very little, going back to my room and then to the bathroom to puke my guts out. I remember lying on the bathroom floor, staring up at the ceiling and thinking, "Man! I have got to go back out there and do this again in an hour and a half."

One option that I did not have was quitting. My older brother, Larry, assured me that he didn't want to see me until Thanksgiving, and I had better be home "just for the weekend" that week. With his admonition in mind, I went back that afternoon and had one of the best practices of my college career. I again had some big hits from my linebacker position and also got my butt nailed at being a tailback. It only took me one day to figure out what side of the ball I needed to be on to be successful in college. After that practice, I was on my way as a college football player. The way I looked at college football after that was if I could make it through that first day, I could make it through anything!

Austin Peay was a good training ground for me as a student and as a budding athlete. I was "redshirted" my freshman year (held out of game playing action during the first year). This was done so that I would have another year of eligibility when I would be bigger and stronger. That all sounded good, but six games into my freshman year of eligibility and despite the fact I had earned a starting position at linebacker, I was suspended from the team for taking a hot plate out of the school cafeteria. You heard right! I was suspended from the team for taking a hot plate from the school cafeteria back to my room to pop popcorn. Grand theft, I guess?

I will always believe that the real reason behind that ridiculous punishment had to do with the fact that my "partner in crime" Ken Reese had busted a knee in the first game of the year; so, this "incident" provided an opportunity for the coaches to eliminate the burden of a guy on full scholarship who would never play again.

It was a gamble on the coach's part that I would come back in the spring. Neither of us returned. We were both better off for it!

After that debacle at Austin Peay, I transferred to Georgia College, back in my hometown of Milledgeville. Georgia College was a small, liberal arts school that had only recently (two quarters before) changed its name from Georgia State College for Women to Georgia College, and the school was admitting males for the first time. When I arrived on campus in 1967, there were approximately 2,000 females on campus and about 300 males, and most of the guys were married. This sounded good, on the surface, but the reason that I transferred back to Georgia College was to get my grades up and gain weight so that I could transfer to a bigger school and fulfill my goal of playing college football again.

In retrospect, Georgia College probably was not a good choice for what I wanted to accomplish. First of all, there were too many girls—a constant distraction—and the guys that transferred to Georgia College were a collection of zany characters that you couldn't believe. These guys were just like me in that they were drawn to this "all of a sudden opportunity" presented by Georgia College. The school accepted males who were either finishing up their degree requirements or needed a stop-off before moving on to a bigger school. Or they could stay put and party their asses off while biding their time at Georgia College.

Milledgeville is a unique southern city. Unlike the typical, small, "Bubba-infested" milltowns so common across the South, Milledgeville is anomaly. It is a white-collar southern town with two colleges, an impressive antebellum history, the Central State Hospital, a regional medical center, several prisons, a technical school, a few industrial plants, and to top all that, a strong tourism industry anchored by Lake Sinclair and the Antebellum Trail.

It's mind-boggling to reflect on the interesting characters this town produced. Mix these guys and girls with the new set of characters brought in by Georgia College and . . . look out!

Dating was a "serious problem." My dad owned a fishing vehicle, a 1954 Ford station wagon that we had dubbed "The Green Leaf Hotel." We would pull that car up in front of the dorms on campus and blow the horn. The girls would just come out and get in. Of course, everyone knew each other. The girls still had an 11:00 p.m. curfew, which was tough to deal with from time to time.

On one occasion, for the spring formal, my buddy Stevie Steverson and I picked up our dates in a chauffeured mule and wagon. We were wearing tuxedos and the ladies were wearing long formal dresses (see "The Wabbit and the Wagon"). The following year, a helicopter was brought in to transport the dates from a banquet at the Holiday Inn to the National Guard Armory where The Tams (a hugely popular band in the '60s through the '90s) were performing. That one didn't work out as well as the first, but it was still a lot of fun.

The good times we had at Georgia College, especially at Lake Sinclair, were special. We once had a big Saturday afternoon party on a small island in the lake we called "Budweiser Island." The party was made up of about fifteen to twenty drunks, but only a couple of boats. We left the island around dark to get back to a cabin on the lake where we had a kick-ass party planned with a bunch of girls from the college. About 9:00 p.m. somebody said, "Has anybody seen 'Fool' or Wallace?" Then it hit us. In our haste to transport people back and forth to the island to get ready for the party, we had left two of our comrades, "Fool" Bradford and Wallace Taylor, out on Budweiser Island. They had been there for the last three hours and were not happy with us when we finally picked them up. Not only had we abandoned them, but we didn't leave them any beer. They were both furious and glad to see us at the same time. Needless to say, they were dressed casually when we got them back to the party.

****

I was in THE Milledgeville Pool Room one day talking to Leroy Herrin, a gentleman for whom I had a lot of respect. Leroy was a fan of mine when I played for Baldwin High and had followed my progress and demise at Austin Peay. "Gary," he asked, "have you considered going to Troy State? They are supposed to be developing a really good football program over there."

I said that I didn't know much about it, but would check into it. I thanked Leroy for his interest, left the pool room, and drove home. As I walked up the steps of my home, I checked the mailbox as an afterthought. In the mailbox was a letter from Troy State University. Unbelievable! The letter was from a coach named Max Howell who said they'd heard from a teammate of mine at Austin Peay about the "raw deal" I got there. They wanted me to come to Troy. I was doing backflips! After receiving the letter, I called Coach Howell, and he invited me to come over to Troy and visit the campus.

My initial visit to Troy State University was both eye-opening and disappointing. My first meeting with Coach Howell was scheduled at the coaches' offices. I showed up and was told to go downstairs where Coach Howell would meet me. There were plenty of pictures on the wall, so I knew what

Coach Howell looked like when he came out of the coaches' offices. But he didn't know what I looked like. As he emerged from his office, I walked over and stuck out my hand.

Howell said, "Excuse me, Son. I'm looking for one of my prospects."

"Who would that be, Coach?" I asked.

"A guy named Gary Spillers," Howell said.

"That would be me, Coach," I beamed.

I have never in my life seen a more disappointed person than Coach Howell that day. After our initial exchange, he sort of blurted out, "YOU are Gary Spillers?"

I guess he was expecting someone a lot bigger; his expression told me he was not pleased with my size. I was 6 feet tall and weighed only 175 pounds.

From that point on, Coach Howell was courteous to me, but not very excited about my prospects. After my initial visit, I got a (save face) letter from the coach, stating that Troy would grant me a full scholarship IF I made the first or second team.

In other words, if I was selected as one of the forty-four players to make first or second team, they would grant me a scholarship. If I came over there and didn't make first or second team, I would be home in a month. I picked up the phone to tell the coach that I would accept his offer. I remember saying, "If I don't make first or second team, I'll be leaving anyway, but don't plan on me leaving!"

I arrived at Troy State University for summer football practice, weighing about 180 pounds. The first thing I noticed when I initially visited Troy was that the Troy players were bigger, stronger, and faster than the Austin Peay players.

As I was getting set up in my room in Alumni Hall, I was assigned to a three-man room with a wide receiver named Jimmy Hedrick, known to everyone as "Cool Head." My other roommate was Jim Gillespie, known to everyone as "Moe." Two better roommates could not have been found.

Our three-bed dorm room was located on the top floor of Alumni Hall, which was reserved only for Troy State football players. Unless they were married, all the players were required to live there. My new roommates had been at Troy for three years: Jimmy, out of LaGrange High School in LaGrange, Georgia, and Moe, a transfer from the University of Georgia who hailed from Clayton, in the mountains of North Georgia. They are still good friends to this day.

One of the first guys I met in Alabama was Lionel Ed Rainey, a transfer from Southern Mississippi, who told me he was from a small Alabama town named "Grainville."

A couple of days later, I was riding around with some other guys when one of them said, "You know that Rainey guy from Greenville is supposed to be a really good player."

I chimed in, "Lionel is not from Greenville; he's from Grainville."

"That's what I said: Greenville," said the other Alabama boy. I had just been given my first lesson in Alabama geography: "Grainville" was actually "Greenville." Hell, what did I know?

The first couple of days of practice at Troy were frustrating for me because we didn't dress out in full gear. It's hard to make an impression as a hard hitter when you are dressed in shorts and jerseys. The third day we dressed in pads for full-contact drills. From that day until the day I graduated, I never worried about whether I could play football at Troy State University. Let's just say I had a good practice.

As my onfield performances were getting better, so were my relationships with my teammates and coaches. The guys at Troy were a wonderful group of close-knit teammates, and once you were accepted as someone who could play and help the team, your social skills seemed to improve as well.

One day, after I had been there about three weeks and was really enjoying the whole atmosphere, really looking forward to the coming football season, our head coach, Billy Atkins, said he needed to talk to me after practice. My heart went to my throat. What was this about? Was he going to let me go, or what?

Coach Atkins met with me after dinner that night and congratulated me on how well I was doing. He said I was doing so well that he had reserved a half scholarship for me when school started. I was stunned. I thought we had a deal for a full ride! He admitted that we did, but that was before they found out I would have to be redshirted.

I said, "Well, Coach, it's been fun. There are some great guys here, and I will miss y'all."

"Do you mean to say you can't stay unless you have a full scholarship?" he asked.

"That's right, Coach. My parents don't have the money to make up the difference. I guess I'll go pack my bags."

"No, you won't," said Coach Atkins, "because you're now on full scholarship."

With that, he turned and walked away without another word.

The whole time I was at Troy, I never signed anything, but I never worried about it after that meeting with Coach Atkins. As it turned out, the coach made a wise choice by not sending me back to Milledgeville. I went from 175 pounds to 215 and became an All-Conference linebacker and a team captain my senior year.

With football being an early success, even though I did have to be redshirted, I was anxious to start classes and see what the women of Troy had to offer. I was hoping that it would not be as bad as Austin Peay, but would be nearly as good as Georgia College. It was better than both combined!

Troy has a very well-developed Greek system that attracts quality ladies, and the Greeks weren't the only source of good-looking ladies—they were everywhere. All of this and Troy was only 100 miles from Panama City Beach. I thought I had died and gone to heaven!

The first year I was enrolled at Troy State University was 1968. Coach Atkins had been hired three years earlier as head coach. He was a former All-American for Auburn University and an All-Pro player for the San Francisco Forty-Niners. Before Coach Atkins arrived, Troy had had a terrible record over fourteen years, with only one winning season.

As all great coaches who are hired to clean up a program, Coach Atkins "cleaned house," getting rid of all the bad to marginal players who had outnumbered the good ones two to one. He then went on the recruiting trail, targeting players who had been dismissed from or had flunked out of larger colleges. Along with his assistant coaches Max Howell and Phillip Creel, Coach Atkins covered the South, giving young men who would work hard a second chance. This approach attracted some high-level talent and some problem kids, too. The coachable, talented kids were groomed for success. The problem kids were shown the door or creatively "run off."

Whatever this guy's strategy was, it worked (I should know; I was one of its beneficiaries). In 1966, Atkins' first year, Troy's record was 5 wins, 5 losses. In 1967, it was 8 wins and 2 losses. In 1968, it was 11 wins, 1 loss. In spite of the loss in 1968, Troy State University made it to a four-team playoff for the National Championship game of the National Association of Intercollegiate Athletics (NAIA). Troy State won the game, beating a heavily favored Texas A&I team in Crampton Bowl in Montgomery, Alabama. It was December 14, 1968.

In 1969, my first year of eligibility, we were 8-1-1. The loss and tie were flukes that never should have happened. This team was probably more talented than the 1968 team, but we lost Al Head, our quarterback, in the first game, and he never fully recovered. We were barred from going to the playoffs because we had two non-winning games. We probably would have won again!

The 1968 team was a special group of guys led by Sim Byrd, a future Alabama Football Hall of Famer. Sim had plenty of help from other stars such as Danny Grant, Vince Green, Bobby Enslen, Ronnie Shelly, George Little, Hugh Cole, Paul Brinsfield, Jim Gillespie, David Cooper, Darwin Fowler, Don Hatcher, Glen Thompson, Rusty Ninas, Larry Grose, and Alvin Dees. Over the years that followed, this group of guys formed a brotherhood that is still intact today.

Another impressive piece of the Troy tradition was the "Sound of the South" Marching Band. Dr. John M. Long had founded the band in 1965 and, during his thirty-two year tenure, worked diligently to establish its national reputation through appearances at music conventions, concert tours, and recordings with the symphony band.

Our band was one of the top college marching bands in the country, not just for small colleges, but for ALL colleges. When the Red Wave hit the practice field in the summer heat, so did the Sound of the South! We were always proud to be represented by this first-class marching band. Dr. Long was just as impressive as Billy Atkins at building a "winner" at Troy. Of course, my favorite part of the band was the majorettes, especially Annette Colley, Kay Farris, Faye Allen, and Joanne Williams.

I have a great memory of sitting in the stands on that cold December day in 1968 at the NAIA National Championship Game. Both teams had cleared the field after warm-ups and were waiting for the National Anthem to begin. After watching both teams warm up, it was obvious that Texas A&I had the superior team, with bigger stronger players. A deadly silence had fallen across the stadium. Only the cold howling December wind could be heard, when a big-winded Texan bellowed from the A&I stands, "Anybody want to bet on Troy?" This was followed by some serious laughter from the A&I side.

There was no retort from the Troy side because we were thinking we could get blown out by this Texas A&I team that had five or six bonafide NFL prospects on their roster. But as they say . . . that's why they play the game. Final score: Troy State University 43; Texas A&I 35!

The game wasn't as close as the score indicated. Sim Byrd and his receivers, Bobby Enslen, Danny Grant, Vince (Boogaloo) Green, and Doug Taylor, bewildered the Texas team's secondary all day long. Halfback Cecil Barber ripped off chunks of yardage at key points in the game and made one 53-yard touchdown that may have been the game-changer. Free safety Ronnie Shelly made three interceptions to lead the defense, and middle linebacker George Little made some vicious tackles along with cornerbacks David Cooper and Darwin Fowler, keeping the powerful Javelinas at bay all afternoon.

Though this Championship Game was a quality contest by two well-prepared teams, it included two of the weirdest football plays I have ever seen in college football. The first was a minus 27-yard punt by Troy punter David Cooper. The wind was blowing hard that day. After receiving the snap from center, David was rushed by a couple of A&I players and hurried his punt from the Troy 28-yard line into the wind. The net effect was that the punt went straight up in the air, got caught by the frigid, gusting wind, rolled backwards, and went out of bounds on Troy's one-yard line.

At half time, thanks to David's punt, the score was tied 21 to 21, and Troy had to kick off to A&I to begin the second half. That's when the second weird play happened. The Javelinas' deep return men were both NFL prospects and could fly. With the aid of the same tailwind that had just cost Troy 6 points before the half, Troy's kicker, Randy Hicks, boomed the kickoff high and deep into the end zone where two A&I players simultaneously attempted to field the ball. One of the receivers caught the ball deep in the end zone, but the other back couldn't pull up in time and knocked his teammate down in the end zone for a safety. Then A&I was forced to kick into the stiff, frigid wind, and the mighty RED WAVE quickly turned that "manna from heaven field position" into 7 points. The rout was on!

"Well, it sure seems that Coach Atkins made the right decision by keeping you on the team. And what a dumb ass that coach at Austin Peay was," said Jenna.

"I agree, Jenna. Dupes was an idiot. I think they fired him two years later. What I learned from the Austin Peay experience is how negative situations can sometimes change your life for the better. When I was suspended from the team at Austin Peay, I thought it was the end of the world. I had lost my scholarship, and my dreams of playing college football were dashed. I had embarrassed myself and my good family name," I recalled.

"I had to put a plan together to get my life back on track so as to complete my dream of finishing up my college career," I lamented. "Georgia College afforded me that chance by taking me in and giving me the opportunity to get my grades up, gain weight, and shop for a football program at another school."

When Troy State came into the picture, it was the opportunity I was looking for, and I made the best of it. In my opinion, Troy State University was a much better school than Austin Peay, and the negative situation at Austin Peay turned out to be one of the best things that ever happened to me.

THE RIVIERA RUN

It was so hot that day, the thermometer belonging to "Jock Itch" (otherwise known as Steve Janckovich, the football team manager) showed 103 degrees in the shade. The Troy State Red Wave was in the middle of summer camp "two-a-days," the tradition of all college football teams to practice twice per day at summer practices. The coaches were bearing down on the players to see who had the guts to stick it out through the torrid late August LA (Lower Alabama) heat.

It was a pretty simple agenda for the coaches. They were in the midst of preparing their veteran players, who had been through this drill before, for a season that held the promise of a championship run. They were also taking a look at the transfers from other schools and the many freshmen, both scholarship players and walk-ons. In other words, the coaches were classifying who was going to be "new meat" for the varsity players to grind up while perfecting their blocking and tackling skills, or who was going to man up and break through the mediocrity to become a bonafide, prospective future player for the Red Wave. It came down to who was going to quit and go home with their tail between their legs, or who was going to stay and become a player.

Quitting the football team during summer practice is not an unfamiliar occurrence at any level of football. At Troy State University every year, seventy to eighty freshmen with scholarships, as well as walk-ons and transfers from other colleges, would show up to participate in summer practice in hopes of making the team. This figure was usually reduced to only ten to fifteen "keepers" by Thanksgiving of each year. Most of these guys were dreamers, "no better than average" high school players who'd probably listened to their mamas, daddies, and/or their high school coaches about how good a football player they were. The dropout ratios were about the same for both freshmen and transfers; for both groups, the lofty dreams of becoming a college football star could quickly dissipate under the blazing South Alabama sun.

When that first whistle blew to begin practice, these former high school stars entered a totally unfamiliar world. All of a sudden, everything changed. The hunter became the hunted. The local star from Wetumpka, Alabama, became just another blocking dummy on the practice field and a basic slave off the field. Tensions mounted even more after practice, as the freshmen were required to shave each other's heads and perform menial tasks at the request of the upper classmen.

It was tough enough to be bullied around for the first time ever during practice, but having to endure it after practice as well was unbearable for most. Many left in the middle of the night, avoiding other players and coaches. Such was the case for Bobby Ennis, a Baldwin High School lineman. Not wanting to confront either coaches or players, he showed up before practice and heaved his high-top cleats and jersey over the fence and hauled ass.

At small schools, scholarships came at a premium because of the limited number available. They were doled out only to producing players; sometimes even injuries, especially season or career-ending injuries, could make it difficult to stay on scholarship. It was the coach's job to weed through the new flock of transfers and freshmen to make sure that the ones who were promised full and partial scholarships were worthy of that elevated status. And if they weren't—to figure out how to bow out of that commitment gracefully, or in some cases, ungracefully. Such was the case in this story.

On this particular 103-degree day, there was no water from Jock Itch. Yep, no water. In the '60s players were not hydrated anywhere near what they are today. To get water at football practice was considered a sign of weakness. Two defensive backs, Lionel Ed Rainey and Joe King, transfers from Southern Mississippi and the University of Alabama, respectively, had just about had enough of the heat and the coaches.

Joe King was a spoiled rich kid from Birmingham, who just couldn't fit into the rigid system and hard practice sessions that Bear Bryant conducted at Alabama. Joe just didn't seem to fit in at Troy, either. It was like he thought it would be easier at Troy. Guess what? To his surprise, it wasn't!

Lionel Ed, on the other hand, wanted to play for the Bear out of high school (what kid in Alabama didn't?), but ended up at Southern Mississippi instead. Lionel Ed was not only a decent defensive back, he had other skills such as punting and serving as a good back-up quarterback. He also was one hell of a golfer. Lionel Ed was ahead of his time. He would have been a great modern-day wildcat formation player. He was really fast. As a matter of fact, one of the more cerebral Troy coaches noted one day in a film session, "Why, that Rainey boy is so fast he could fart in a deer's face!"

Joe approached Lionel Ed on the sideline during another waterless heat break and said, "I don't know about you, but I'm thinking about getting the hell out of Dodge. This heat is killing me, and I'm not so sure this place is for me anyway. Plus, there's a bunch of hot blonde babes down at Panama City Beach (i.e., the Redneck Riviera) at the end of summer parties, just waiting for me and you and my new 442."

Joe now had Lionel Ed's attention. First, the mere mention of a big-tittied bleached blonde bounding down the beach rung Lionel Ed's bell. Second, showing up in Joe's 442 would certainly increase their chances of landing said big-tittied bleached blonde in the sack, possibly even before the night was over.

The scent of the hunt for a well-endowed blonde was just too much for Lionel Ed. He blurted, "Shit, Joe, I'm in! I don't like this place much either. When do you want to go?"

"Let's skip the supper training table so while everyone else is eating, we'll haul ass." said Joe.

Done deal! The two desperados were on their way to the Redneck Riviera.

That afternoon, as their teammates were having dinner, Joe and Lionel Ed loaded all their earthly possessions into Joe's car and got the hell out of Dodge. They took the Redneck Riviera beach route: US Highway 231 South out of Troy down through Brundidge, Enterprise, and Dothan and on to the Riviera. Or so they thought!

Joe's 442 was humming as they cruised by Brundidge and then through Dothan. That was about the time Lionel Ed's first guilt pangs began to set in. He was a good kid from a good family in Greenville, Alabama (pronounced "Grainville" by many locals), and was the youngest of three successful brothers who supported his every move, except maybe this one. What would they say? Lionel Ed hadn't factored in what his brothers would think of this hasty decision. What would his mom and dad say? "Oh shit, have I screwed up or what? Have I let the blood in my brain drain to my dick and cloud my thinking?"

It was just a little south of Dothan when the Riviera Run began to unravel and Lionel Ed's fortunes changed for the better! Joe was cruising just a little over the speed limit when the blue lights (may have still been red lights at that time) flashed in the rearview mirror.

Joe slowed the car and cautiously pulled over to the side of the road as the Alabama state trooper pulled in behind the 442. The larger-than-life trooper approached the vehicle, bent over, looked into the 442, and without asking for a driver's license barked, "Are you Joe King?"

"Yes sir!" stammered Joe.

Looking past Joe, the trooper said, "Are you Lionel Ed Rainey?"

Lionel Ed gulped, "Yes sir."

The trooper then said, "Rainey, get your shit out of the back of this car and put it in the back of my car. Coach Atkins said it was time you got your ass back to Troy!"

Lionel Ed bolted from his seat and began unloading his Riviera-bound belongings from Joe's 442 as the big trooper stood by silently supervising the move. Finally, Joe couldn't stand it anymore and got up the nerve to ask the trooper, "Sir, what did Coach Atkins say about me?"

"I am glad you asked that question because I have been instructed by Coach Atkins to tell you to keep on going!" He turned to Lionel Ed, "Load up, Rainey!"

One scholarship saved. One questionable player gone!

"Wow, those coaches could get tough sometimes, couldn't they?" inquired Lindy.

"Yes," I said, "they could. You just had to make sure you were always in their good graces or your ass would be gone, too," I said. If the coaches believed in you as player and a student they would do anything in their power to help you.

"One time, me, Jim Duncan and a couple of other players were sitting in my car at the local hang-out in Troy, The Dairy Delight, run by our good friend W.C. Watkins, when some soldiers from Fort Rucker rode through and gave us the finger and yelled something at us. We didn't like that at all, so we decided to chase them down and 'bring them to justice.' To make a long story short, we ended up rear-ending the soldiers' car with my car. Before it was all over, the charges were reversed through the help of a couple of attorneys, Nick Cervera and Joel Folmer, to charge the soldiers with illegally blocking a lane of traffic!

"These coaches have a tough job and limited funds to work with at a small school. Plus they have to deal with free spirits like Lionel Ed Rainey and me," I said. "We were always into something like in the case of this next tale, 'The Carriage Inn Caper.'"

THE CARRIAGE INN CAPER

It was the summer of my junior year at Troy State University. I was attending summer school and working in Troy at the Coca Cola plant, doing odd jobs. My roommate for the summer, Lionel Ed Rainey, was working with the State Highway Department, heading up the dead dog patrol. I'm not making this up. Lionel said that they got to sleep on the side of the road a lot, but when they were awake, it did sometimes get messy.

Both positions held very promising training advantages for our futures. We were renting a two-bedroom trailer from a friend for the summer and had a pretty good set-up for two college boys. I was home studying one night when Lionel came bursting into the trailer with an offer I couldn't refuse. It seemed that Lionel had been out to the Carriage Inn (a local dive on Highway 231, just north of town) the night before and had met two blondes who, according to Lionel Ed, were hot and wanted to meet us there tonight. It sounded too good to be true. First of all, Lionel Ed loved blondes, but he was not particularly keen on their looks past, say, the blonde hair line. I, on the other hand, was a little more selective with my women. But Lionel Ed was assuring me that I would like these girls, and of course they were "hot."

There was one thing for sure: studying in the middle of the summer was no fun. So I quizzed Lionel a little more about these babes and, for once, he was coming up with the right answers. I still didn't feel good about this deal, but what the hell, I thought, let's give it a shot.

We headed out in Lionel Ed's 1962 Chevy clunker and got to the Inn a little early as the band was just setting up. Everything seemed cool, and a few people were beginning to filter in as the band started to play. It was then and there that the two blonde bombshells actually did show up. The only problem was, both of them had guys attached to them.

"Shit!" Lionel spat out. "They told me they were not going to be with those guys again tonight."

"Lionel Ed, do you mean to tell me that you drug me all the way out here tonight to meet girls who already have dates? And pretty big dates I might add," I said.

"Well, they said they would be alone tonight. The lying bitches!" grumbled Lionel Ed.

The band began to play, and the blondes weren't giving Lionel Ed the time of day, but their boyfriends were. I could tell something was going on, but I couldn't tell what. Apparently, the ladies had told Lionel Ed that they would meet him, but then got caught by their boyfriends. And now that they were caught, it looked like they were covering their asses and blaming everything on Lionel Ed. When the music started, the two couples went out of their way to dance directly in front of our table, and the girls were shaking their asses right in Lionel's face, taunting him. The boyfriends thought that was all kind of cute. So I made a wise crack. "Take it all off, Baby."

The one blonde wheeled around and said, "You ain't got enough money to make me take it off, Buddy!"

"We'll see about that," I said. I then flipped a quarter out onto the dance floor and said, "Here is a quarter, but I damn sure want some change back."

This gesture did not sit well with our blonde friends and their boyfriends. It was like they went into a football huddle at their table; every once in a while, a head would pop up and look our way. We just sat there to see what would happen next. After a few minutes, the smaller of the two guys, about Lionel Ed's size, got up and headed over to our table and asked Lionel Ed to step outside. It seemed they'd already had words the night before, another fact Lionel Ed had failed to reveal to me.

Lionel Ed stood up and headed outside when it hit me that this guy might have a knife or even a gun. I got up and walked over to the table where the blonde bimbos were sitting with the other guy and told him that I didn't like my friend being outside alone, and I was going out there and if he would like to join me, to bring his ass on. As I walked outside, the big boy followed me out.

I found Lionel standing at the corner of the building when I got outside. I said, "Lionel Ed, get back over here. If these sons of bitches want to fight, we are going to do it in the light, not in some alley."

Then over my shoulder, I heard the big boy say, "You are shit!"

I turned and said, "What did you say?"

"You are sh . . . ," but he never got the rest out. I hit him square in the mouth and knocked him up on the hood of a car, hit him again as he rolled off the car, then kicked him in the teeth as he started to get up. The big boy was done for the day after that exchange. I looked at Lionel Ed and said we needed to get going, and we did.

As we jumped into Lionel Ed's car, the first guy, seeing his henchman had been destroyed, walked to his car and started opening his trunk.

"Get this thing cranked! That guy is going for his gun!" I said.

Lionel Ed was trying to crank the old Chevy, but it just wouldn't fire. The engine was going "waraugh-waraugh" with no ignition fire. Then, the guy came out of his trunk—not with a gun, but something just as deadly, a bumper jack! He began swinging it around and headed for our car. The old Chevy was still sitting there, going waraugh . . . waraugh, with the starter barely turning over. We were sitting ducks!

The guy approached our car and wildly swung the jack at the windshield, knocking the radio antenna off the car. I saw an opening where I thought I could get to the guy before he could do any more damage. I pushed the door open and tried to jump out of the car and, as I did, Lionel Ed's car cranked up and lunged backward, the open door knocking me down in the parking lot.

So there I was, in the parking lot with the crazed guy holding the bumper jack, who was now starting to chase me with the deadly weapon. If this wasn't a live reenactment of a keystone cops type of scene, I don't know what was. I began shuffling backwards across the parking lot with Lionel trying to maneuver the car between me and the guy with the bumper jack. All of a sudden, I backed up onto a pile of bricks, which I immediately began throwing toward the guy. After a couple of direct hits, I actually started chasing him. Lionel Ed saw the opening and shot between us in the old Chevy. I jumped in and we hauled ass, leaving the slightly disoriented warrior with his bumper jack and his pummeled friend still lying in the parking lot wondering what the hell just happened!

As we were going down the road, I put a "dog cussing" on Lionel Ed for getting me into that mess. Lionel Ed took it like a man. He was duly remorseful, apologized for his error in judgment, and promised me he would never let such an aggressive transgression of my civil rights ever take place again. Then with his evil little giggle, he added, "Hee . . . hee . . . hee. Wanna check out the lounge at the Holiday Inn for some babes . . . on the way home?"

The Gateway to The West!
The St. Louis Gateway Arch

Stacy Evans, Miss Florida 1973

Little Tommy Arrington!
How innocent can you look?

Troy State University's "Sound of the South," the best
college marching band in the world! Directed by the
legendary Dr. Johnny Long

THE Milledgeville Poolroom / Early '70s Georgia College mini-reunion group (left to right): Terri Head, Gary Spillers, Becky Smith, Dodo Hollis, Lisa Bell, David Lord, and Julie Clark

Gary Spillers, Troy's team captain and All-Conference linebacker, "hucking and bucking" for Laughead photographers.

Visiting the lovely Ms. Julie Clark at Jacksonville Beach with one of my teammates Mike Caldwell and Becky Smith. Notice the premium beer!

The Pig makes it to Colorado! Pikes Peak, Colorado

Jenna Stubbs and friends at the Hotel Jerome. Jimmy Buffett dropped by later that day.

Blackjack game in Delta, Utah

Aspen Mountain

One of the many clowns at the Aspen Snow Dance

Gary Spillers with Maroon Bells in the background

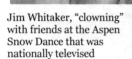

Jim Whitaker, "clowning" with friends at the Aspen Snow Dance that was nationally televised

The Domino Lounge, famous Downtown Atlanta "Den of Iniquity." Note the name of the featured dancer.

Jack Maddox and Larry Eady in the front seats and "Alert" Eddie Powell and Gary Spillers in the back

J. "Moe" Gillespie, dancing with the stars at Mardi Gras

The Troy State University 1971 Homecoming Court: Fay Allen (seated) reigned as Homecoming Queen. Members of the Homecoming Court were (left to right) Janet Wilkinson, Pat Trawick, and Jackie Coker.

Pit Stops…er, I mean Pig Stops along the way

1- Atlanta-Ground Zero;   2- First stop-over, St. Louis, Missouri;   3- The encounter with the Colorado Kid;   4- Colorado Springs. The Pig makes it to Colorado and Pikes Peak;   5- Independence Pass;   6- Vail and Alfred Packer;   7- The awesome mecca of Aspen, Colorado;

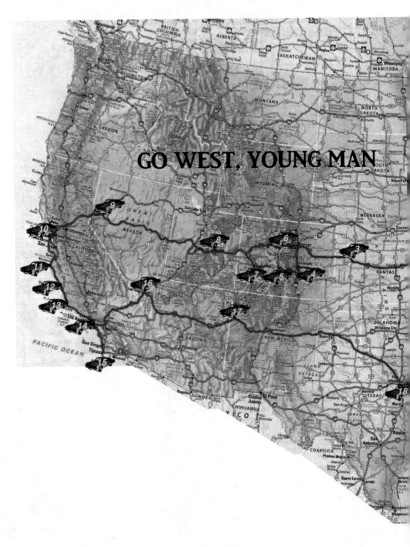

8- Delta, Utah; 9- Lake Tahoe; 10- San Francisco; 11- Monterrey Peninsula; 12- Carmel; 13- The Fabulous California Highway One; 14- Los Angeles; 15- Tijuana, Mexico; 16- Las Vegas...uh-oh!; 17- Desert Police in New Mexico...uh-oh again!; 18- The Dallas Cowboys' play-off dud! Would you believe three uh-ohs in a row?

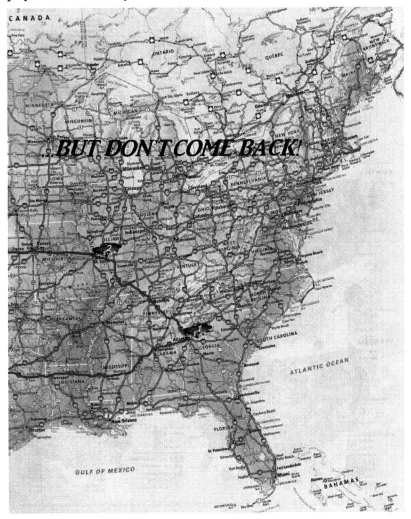

The motorhome road trip to Mardi Gras. Left to right: Cheryl Majors, Jack Smith, Jim Gillespie with the latest designer nosepiece, and Tom Majors. Having fun after a scrumptious meal at Commander's Palace in New Orleans.

"Cool Head" Hedrick— the most level-headed guy on campus. Cool Head said this was the closest he got to a textbook while at Troy.

"Whoa . . . Coach! What language are you speaking in? (Lionel Ed gets instructions from Coach Atkins.)

Gary Spillers, threatening to be arrested for putting on a local cop's hat in a New Orleans restaurant

Famous Atlanta landmark dance club Johnny's Hideaway on Roswell Road

Meeting up with
our hippie
"chauffeurs" on
Bourbon Street

Gary Spillers
and the
Golden Gate
Bridge

Waves crashing
against the
Monterey
Peninsula

Celebrating reaching the
Pacific Ocean (left to right):
Bryna McNeely, Gary Spillers,
Jenna Stubbs, and Lindy
Stevens

Hollywood Boulevard in
Hollywood, California

Bill "Boy" Harrington chats
with Larry "Snake "Spillers
about global affairs and the
political atmosphere of the
world as they see it! In the
background are Rhett
Harrison, Hunter Bacon, and
host Jack Maddox at a Wall
brothers "pickin' and
grinnin'" concert.

Dinner in Tijuana, Mexico. Billy
Cordoza and Gary seem to be
outnumbered by senoritas,
but they struggled their way back
to the border in spite of it all!

Gary and Cheryl in
Tijuana, Mexico. Most
guys take their women
to Cabo. Maybe that
was the problem?

Left to right: Old teammates Gary Spillers, Johnny Cowart, and "the one and only" Lionel Ed Rainey from "Grainville," Alabama.

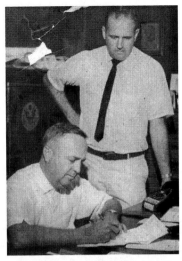

Freddy Layton, director of the Milledgeville Recreation Department (standing) with long-time mayor of Milledgeville Walter B. Williams, Jr.—two juggernauts of Milledgeville history in the late '50s and through the '60s.

The Stardust Hotel in Las Vegas. Cheap lodging that I never saw after changing clothes there.

The Pig makes it to the Pacific.

The Dallas Cowboys' play-off dud! Check out the price of this NFL play-off ticket.

"The Plowboy Cowboys" - Old Milledgeville buddies.
Harold Thomkins and Bill Sibley in front. In the rear, Hector Mendez (with the mysterious object), and Drew and Nicky Santarone. Reprinted from The Spectrum, Georgia College's 1972 yearbook.

Beautiful Downtown Milledgeville, Georgia's shopping and dining area. The Downtown area sits between the college campuses of Georgia College and State University and Georgia Military College.

CHAPTER FIVE

The back side of Nevada on Highway 50, a two-lane road, was plenty boring, especially at night. Though the Toiyabe Range and the Shoshone Mountains were beautiful at night, we were pushing hard for Lake Tahoe by noon the next day. It looked like we would have no trouble making our goal until it started blowing snow about an hour outside of Lake Tahoe. Lindy was driving at the time, so I volunteered to take over the reins and get us into Lake Tahoe. It was a good thing I did. About fifteen minutes outside of Lake Tahoe, a strange thing happened.

It was blowing snow pretty much level with the ground and beginning to ice up pretty fast. To complicate things even further, local traffic in Lake Tahoe was building in anticipation of the mountain storm moving in. We had cars in front of us and behind as well when it happened. I don't know if we hit a slick spot or what, but all of a sudden the Green Pig went into a 360-degree tail spin and ended up back on the road with the same car in front of us and the same car behind us, as if nothing had happened! Everybody in the car just looked at each other, shook their heads, and patted the ole Green Pig's dashboard in appreciation for saving our lives once again.

Lake Tahoe was a beautiful place and, after a drive out to see the Lake's sites, a few hands of blackjack, and some slot machine action on the girls' part (except for Lindy), we chose to hit the road again and headed for San Francisco, a mere 220 miles west. San Fran, here we come! The Pig has made it to Colorado and through the badlands of Utah and Nevada. Now to California! Raise the Golden Gate, we are a-coming!

We hadn't been on the road long before the girls needed their story fix, so I shared a few more stories about college life and my Troy State experiences. Probably my favorite story about Lionel Ed Rainey and his wild times down at Troy is "Daince Me by the Window."

DAINCE ME BY THE WINDOW

It was early September, and the Troy State University Red Wave had just finished two-a-day practices (the barbarian ritual of practicing twice a day during summer preseason training camp). The team was rounding itself into shape for taking yet another Gulf South Conference Football title or, possibly, another national championship run.

The team had been going through college football's version of Marine boot camp, and we were ready for some action, as in girl action. It was a good two weeks before the majority of students would arrive at school, and we were looking for some type of female entertainment. Troy, Alabama, in the summer of 1969 was no place to be without the other students, as in GIRLS.

One of my runnin' buddies Lionel Ed Rainey came up with some reliable information on a place that was supposed to really rock on Saturday nights down in a little town called Brundidge, Alabama, just ten miles south of Troy. Although Lionel Ed's information wasn't always that accurate, especially about joints and women, this place called Dykes Club sounded pretty good.

We decided to try it out. Running the risk that we might run into a bunch of redneck girls wearing bermuda-alls (cut-off overalls) didn't deter us one bit. We had been trapped for two weeks with a bunch of jocks, and we were ready for anything. The scouting report said that it was a country and western joint with a good band, and there usually were some fairly attractive single women available to dance with.

That Saturday night, Jack Smith, Lionel Ed, and I headed out for Brundidge and the Dykes Club. On the way down, Lionel Ed had a couple of beers, and when the subject changed to women, Lionel Ed began his evil-sounding little giggle. "Hee . . . hee . . . hee . . . ! You guys know that between the three of us we, have pretty much had every girl that is available at Troy. Hee . . . hee . . . hee! Spillers, you and Jack have had all the good-looking ones and . . . I have had all the ugly ones!"

As we pulled into the parking lot, nothing seemed much different than any country and western joint that I had been in before. The gravel parking lot, the presence of more trucks than cars, the neon beer and whiskey signs, the concrete block structure with the big fold-up wooden windows that folded out and up to get plenty of fresh air to the dancers . . . all were standard fixtures on warm weather nights similar to this Saturday night.

Of course, there was the 300-pound gorilla taking cover charges, sitting next to the sign that strictly said, "Leave all guns and knives outside." Heck, I went into a joint one time that was so rough its sign said, "If you don't have a gun or knife, please contact the manager and, according to your particular needs, he will get you one or both!"

After we made it through security and got inside, the music sounded really good, plus the inside looked surprisingly clean and comfortable. Jack suggested that we split up so we wouldn't look too conspicuous, you know, like a bunch of college students or something stupid like that. We all agreed. Lionel Ed already had a bleached blonde in his sights, and he was off to the races. Jack went one way and I went the other, but not before we obtained a promise from Lionel Ed that he wouldn't run off with some dirty leg and screw us up from getting back to the dorm by bed check time. (I told you summer practice was like boot camp.)

I wandered off through the huge building that comprised a main bar, a country and western band area, and a square dance area. As I walked into the country band section, I spotted a pretty young lady sitting by herself at a table. I approached her and asked her if she would like to dance. She turned around in her chair and looked me over from head to toe.

"You ain't from around here, are ya?" she asked.

"I kinda am. I go to school up at Troy."

She then looked me over again and downed the rest of her bourbon and coke. "It don't matter none to me, and I don't care where you're from, 'cause I don't daince like these hicks down here anyway. I daince modern!"

"Well good, then," I said. "Let's do some modern daincing!"

"I'm in, Big Boy. Let's go!"

For those of you who have never experienced asking a country girl to dance in a country and western club, please be aware that they begin dancing when they leave their chair. They dance around and through the tables on the way to the dance floor. This lady was no different. And to make that trip dancing through the tables and chairs just to find out what dancing modern is like was worth it. I found out soon enough. As my partner cleared the last table and reached the edge of the dance floor, she jumped for what looked like 10 feet in the air, did a perfect 180-degree body twist, landed on her feet, and started to pump her straight arms wildly, up and down— similar to the old "hully gully" dance we did in high school. Not knowing what to do and surely not wanting to embarrass my dance partner, I made a similar jump move and hit the floor, pumping my arms like her and doing some serious modern daincing.

After several modern dainces, a couple of drinks, some highly intellectual conversations about her favorite soap opera stars and the things that those people do to each other, plus what was going on with the careers of her favorite wrestler Freddie Blassie and stock car racer "Fireball" Roberts, I was thoroughly informed. I had about all the fun I could have at one time, so I excused myself, thanked my partner for the modern daince lessons, and went looking for Jack and Lionel Ed.

Jack was easy to find, but as usual, Lionel Ed wasn't. According to Jack, "The last time I saw Lionel Ed, he was 'luved up' on some woman that looked like she was 70 years old and they were square dancing their asses off."

"Oh shit!" I said. "I hope he hasn't left because Lionel Ed can't afford to miss curfew, or his ass will be history!"

As Jack and I combed the square dance room, we found Lionel Ed over in the corner with his new senior citizen friend. Not that Lionel Ed was, or wasn't, a big fan of older women, but he did once admit to getting a little "woozy" one night in Birmingham and went home with this lady, only later to wake up on the sofa by himself, staring at a glass of water on the coffee table with a set of false teeth soaking in it.

We usually have to drag Lionel Ed kicking and screaming away from situations like this, but this time he popped up and said, "You guys ready to go?"

As we were heading for the door, Lionel Ed thanked us for rescuing him.

"I knew the old girl was a little up in age, but hell, you guys know I have developed a low cull factor. You know what I always say . . . go ugly early . . . save money!" He continued, "Do y'all remember that last square dance? Well, as I was dancing with my partner, she gave me a big hug, then looked deep into my eyes and said, 'Lionel Ed, Baby . . . will you please daince me by the window where I can spit?'"

Vintage Lionel Ed!

"Eueee . . . !"All the girls screamed almost in unison.

"There must have been quite a few characters down at Troy," said Jenna.

"You are correct, Mademoiselle, and you may remember that is where your good friend Tommy Arrington is from. Not only did he go to school there, but he was from Troy, Alabama. There is no telling what kind of trouble we would have gotten into on this trip if he'd been along," I said.

Tommy Arrington was one wildman in his college days. We were not close friends, or even friends at all, because we dated the same girl. Susan would play us against each other and bounce back and forth between us at her whim. After she finally ditched both of us, which was the smartest thing she ever did, Tommy and I became friends, and all hell broke loose!

I went over to pick Tommy up one night and blew the horn, and he didn't come out of his apartment. I don't remember what made me look up, but when I did, there stood Tommy on top of his apartment house butt ass nekkid. It was dark and that was a good thing, because if it wasn't, he would have surely been arrested! Well maybe not. Lack of evidence . . . if you know what I mean!

Tommy was the number one singles player on the Troy State Tennis Team. He had two pretty sisters, Suzanne and Christy, who also attended Troy State.

PROS THEY WERE

Two of my favorite teammates and buddies at Troy State University were Jack Smith and Jim "Moe" Gillespie. Jack hailed from the Southeastern Georgia town of Ocilla, and Jim was from about as northeast as you can get—up in the mountains around Clayton. Both were "pros." Jack became a professional football player for the Philadelphia Eagles, and Jim became a pro-duce man, raising cabbage for a living!

The three of us had always talked about going to Mardi Gras together, but for various reasons we never did. So two years after we graduated, we put together a trip that involved my renting a motorhome in Georgia, meeting them in Troy, Alabama, and then heading down to New Orleans.

I had a buddy in Milledgeville at that time, Jerry McCommon, who owned a motorhome and agreed to rent it to me for four or five days at a fair price. I got all packed up and headed out to meet the pros in Troy on a Friday afternoon. The motorhome was nice. It had a generator and sleeping capacity of six with indoor toilets and everything. Man, we were traveling in luxury!

We were to meet in Troy at Lefty's Bar, the number one hangout for most of the jocks at Troy when we were there. It was owned by Lefty Green, a crafty old veteran who knew how to treat college kids, as well as how to make money on them. Lefty was getting on up in age and had just recently sold the bar to Jack and a partner named Leonard Casey. Jack financed the deal with money from his signing bonus with the Philadelphia Eagles. Leonard was to be the year-round managing partner because of Jack's long season in pro football.

****

As I was driving down to Troy in the motorhome, many memories flooded my mind about Lefty's Bar. I was a pretty good pool hustler in college, and Lefty had both pool tables and bowling machines to gamble on that provided beer money every once in a while and a loss of funds from time to time as well.

One longstanding tradition at Lefty's was that if you graduated (and many of Lefty's student-customers did not graduate, for obvious reasons), you were allowed to sign the back wall of the bar. When Jim Gillespie and I graduated, we went straight to Lefty's and wrote on the wall in large letters "J. Moe Gillespie and G. Bruce Spillers has graduated 12-13-1970. There's hope for everyone!"

Gillespie and I already had jobs lined up in South Carolina with Deering-Milliken, the textile giant. But we had to visit each plant where we would work to make it official. So after signing the wall at Lefty's and leaving our Troy legacies behind in the rearview mirror, we were off to Spartanburg, South Carolina.

After completing the road trip to Carolina and being assigned plants to work in, we returned to our homes, me to Milledgeville and Jim to Clayton. On the following Monday, I got a call from Gillespie. "Spools (one of my nicknames)," he said, "I got bad news this morning. I didn't graduate!"

Apparently, Jim had flunked a course that he thought he passed. He was devastated and afraid that Deering-Milliken was going to renege on his job offer, but they didn't, and we both went to work for them in South Carolina. Neither one of us lasted six months. The textile business was not for us. I went into construction, and Jim returned to Troy to finish his one course and to be a graduate assistant football coach, later becoming "Cabbage Head" world champion cabbage grower. A real pro!

My favorite memory of Lefty Green happened one night as several adventurous couples were partying and playing our favorite coed game called "Gotcha" at our apartment. Gotcha was a spin-off of the popular board drinking game of that period called "Pass Out," which was a drinking game modeled after Monopoly. Except we changed the rules and the board so that when a player rolled the dice and landed on a certain spot, he or she had to take a shot, chug a beer, or drink something. Every other spot, however, directed the player to do something a little vulgar like exchange an article of clothing with your date, fanny bite to the right, or kiss someone else's date. In other words, every one ended up getting shit-faced and half naked (if not all the way).

One night as the Gotcha game was in full swing, a terrible thing happened. We ran out of beer! I volunteered to go to Lefty's to get more beer. The only problem was my date had on my clothes, and I had on most of hers. No problem, we went anyway!

As we walked into the bar, I sporting my date's bra and panties and she with my shirt and pants on, Lefty himself stopped what he was doing to wait on us.

"Lefty," I said, "Go get me a case of beer quick. Time's a wastin'. We need to git back to the party!"

Lefty went to the beer cooler, promptly returned with two cases of beer, and said, "Gary, I ain't never seen anything like this in my bar in the twenty years I been here. Lord! If I could be young like you just one more time! One of the cases is on me! Y'all have fun."

****

The original plan was to meet Jack and Jim at the bar, have a couple of beers, and take off for New Orleans with arrival time projected around midnight, just in time to party. Noble plans are made to be broken, aren't they?

I pulled up at Lefty's around 5:00 p.m., and the place was hopping. Not only was it happy hour, but a pool tournament was scheduled to get under way any minute, with the winner getting five cases of beer. Jack had already registered me in the tournament, thinking I may be able to win some beer or money for the trip. Three hours later and many beers consumed, I won the pool tournament.

So, with a good stock of beverages, a decent amount of cash from side-bets, and Jack's and Jim's bags loaded into the motorhome, we said goodbye to the well-wishers at

Lefty's and off we went, down Highway 29 toward Luvern, Greenville, and I-65 South to "The Big Easy" and New Orleans. Five to six miles out of Troy, however, the motorhome's engine started to spit, cough, and sputter. With all the hoopla going on, I had forgotten to fill up for the trip. We had just run out of gas!

Add another good hour or two for getting refueled and we were back on the road again, finally on our way at about the time that we had originally planned to arrive. No problem, we weren't on a time clock. None of us were married, so we didn't have to report in to anyone, and we sure as hell didn't have to worry about getting a hotel room—Hell, we were driving it!

Almost as soon as we got on the road good, a poker game broke out! We were motoring down Highway 29, and Jim was dealing cards on the serving tables between the driver's seat and front passenger seat. I was driving and playing my hand at the same time and not doing a very good job of either. Something had to give. No one wanted to drive, but we didn't want to impede our progress after we had finally had gotten on the road and were making some concerted effort to move in a southerly direction.

We pulled into Luverne, a small town in LA (Lower Alabama). The street lights of downtown gave off a dull, yellowish glow as our traveling casino knifed its way through the darkness of Highway 29. All of a sudden, I spotted two hippies hitchhiking. At first, I paid them no attention, Then, Voila! Could they be potential drivers? Maybe! I hit the brakes and pulled over.

The hippies came sprinting up to the motorhome. They knew their chances of getting a ride this late at night were almost zero, and they were thankful for any transportation opportunity. Jack rolled his window down and asked, "Y'all wouldn't be headed to Madri Gras, would you?"

They both replied, "Yes, yes we are. Are y'all?"

I took over from there and queried, "Do you guys have a valid driver's license?"

They both said, "Yes, we both do."

"Let me see 'em," I said.

I checked them out. They were both from Montgomery and, according to their story, were hitchhiking to Mardi Gras.

"Can you guys drive this rig?" I asked. They both were certain that they could.

"Well, get in and let's see . . . if you can handle it, you got a ride all the way to Canal Street. If you can't, your asses will be out at the next street corner."

Both hippies ended up being excellent drivers. In other words, they didn't wreck the motorhome in the first two blocks. As soon as the driving tests were over, we immediately resumed our poker game as one of our heavily bearded chauffeurs took over the reins.

Impromptu poker games have always taken place in the strangest locations. My old friend Alex Hawkins, while playing for Don Shula and the Baltimore Colts, was busted by the Baltimore cops for playing poker in the back of a barber shop in Baltimore at 4:30 in the morning. As Shula was dressing down "the Hawk" for getting busted, he said, "Alex, did you know that a couple of those guys you were busted with have long criminal records?"

Alex replied, "Well, Coach, it's hard enough to get a poker game going in a barber shop at that time of the morning. We just didn't have time to get a background check on all the players."

Neither did we with our hippies. "Look out Mardi Gras, here we come!" we thought.

We arrived in New Orleans just after daylight and, as promised, dropped off our hippies on Canal Street. We then went looking for a place to park and ended up next to St. Louis Cemetery Number 1, an old cemetery made famous by the movie *Easy Rider*. How can you beat a room with a cemetery view? Especially this cemetery!

As soon as we got parked, we took a four- or five-hour nap, then got dressed to go attack Bourbon Street and all it had to offer—which was plenty, even for me and my "pros." As we reached Bourbon Street and the French Quarter, the first couple of people we saw were our hippies. We bought them a drink and have never seen them again in this lifetime.

Our first night was fairly uneventful as far as Mardi Gras goes, other than Gillespie out-dancing all the street kids and old men dancers. Apparently, they had never seen a North Georgia hillbilly clog (or buck dance) before! We did the usual Hurricanes at Pat O'Brien's, Oysters at The Pearl, shooters at several establishments, and were threatened by a cop with his billy club for trying on his helmet after he had hung it on a hat rack at a restaurant.

Runnin' wild on Bourbon Street reminded me of the old song by Doug Clark and the Hot Nuts: "We were walking down Canal Street docking on every door . . . . It got damp and something bit you, we couldn't find a door." It sounds ridiculous, but sing that lyric real fast, and you will figure it out. Ole Doug died in 2002, God rest his soul. His band was well known in the '60s by most universities in the South. They were great (off color/slightly risqué) entertainers.

The next day was much like the first, but that afternoon before going out on the town, we paid a visit to Jim's old high school sweetheart, Cheryl Majors, who had married and was living in New Orleans with her husband, Tom. Feeling sorry for us and our squalid living quarters, Cheryl invited us over to their apartment to take a hot shower and clean up before going out to dinner with her and her husband. None of us had met Tom who had been out of town and was due back that afternoon.

Jack and I were to take a shower first in the slightly cramped, one-bedroom apartment. As we were in the process of unpacking our clothes, Jim stuck his head in and announced that he and Cheryl were going to make a run to the local beverage store. I was in the process of shaving and Jack was in the shower. Almost as soon as Jim closed the door and left with Cheryl, the door popped back open, and a total stranger was standing there with travel bags under both arms. Assuming that this was Tom and that he had met Jim and Cheryl in the hallway, I continued to shave with nothing on but a towel. Jack was still in the shower. So, the man asked, "Where is my wife?"

I jokingly replied, "She's in the shower."

The man slammed his bags down, went back into the living room, then came back into the bedroom and said, "Who the hell are you? And where is my wife?"

Then it hit me. He had not met Jim and Cheryl in the hallway, he really didn't know who I was, and he was probably about to shoot me and his "wife" in the shower!

I began spitting out everything I could to make sure I got him calmed down. I said, "Did you not meet Jim Gillespie and Cheryl on the way out? No, that is not your wife in the shower. That is my buddy Jack Smith. Cheryl invited us over to take a shower before dinner tonight, and she and Jim went to pick up some snacks and beverages. Are we okay now?"

Finally, Tom smiled and said everything was fine, but I had him going when I made the remark about Cheryl being in the shower. Apparently, Jim had taken the motorhome to the beverage store. So when Tom got home, Cheryl's car was in the driveway and everything seemed normal, except for a total stranger standing in his bathroom with nothing on but a towel, with the shower running behind him!

After Jim and Cheryl got back, we all had a good laugh about the whole misunderstanding. We then took the motorhome to an old classic restaurant, Commander's Palace, where we had dinner, and a good time was had by all.

It was brought up at dinner that for my remark to Tom about his wife being in the shower, I should receive the "Dickhead of the Year" award. It was officially voted on, and I was presented a very prestigious set of horn-rimmed glasses with a penis as a nosepiece. I have never been more proud!

Three nights in a cramped motorhome in New Orleans is enough for anyone, so the next day we headed back, but not before we did one more drive through the French Quarter, searching desperately for our hippies to no avail. We even remembered to refuel this time before leaving.

"What a great way to go to Mardi Gras!" said Lindy. I agreed that it was a "hoot," but I don't think I would attempt it again unless I had my "hippies" booked in advance. Lindy just had to chip in that I should still have the "dickhead" glasses to wear every day.

"Would y'all like to hear about another trip originating in Troy that me and some of my buddies got involved in that, let's just say, was interesting?"

BEACHED IN MIAMI . . . LYNCOACH STYLE

I was headed over to the Troy State University Post Office one morning when I ran into one of our football coaches, Max Howell. He had a stranger with him that I didn't recognize. Coach Howell called me over and introduced the guy as Bob Sanders, the personnel director of the Lyncoach Trucking Company. Lyncoach was a large outfit located in Troy, out on the Montgomery Highway. Their main business was building the bodies for rental truck fleets such as Avis, Ryder, and U-Haul.

Coach Howell said, "Gary, Bob here is looking for a group of drivers to deliver thirty Ryder trucks to Miami this weekend from Troy. They will pay you 250 dollars to drive one of their trucks to Miami, and they will furnish you transportation back to Troy. They are looking for guys who need to make some money this weekend. Do you want to sign up, and do you think you can help Bob recruit some other drivers?"

I said, "I am definitely in, and I think "Cool Head" (Jim Hedrick, my roommate in the football dorm) and "Slimey" Spikes will go, too."

Slimey was a neat buddy of ours from Phenix City, Alabama, who had earned the respect of Cool Head and some of the other football players on the first day of class. The professor had done something totally foreign to college students: seating everyone in alphabetical order. He then started calling the roll, using everyone's formal names, but he graciously asked each student if they had a preferred nickname.

When he called "James Gillespie," Jim answered, "Teach, everyone just calls me Moe."

The professor acknowledged that request, then called "Hugh C. Hendricks," and the response was, "Sir, everyone just calls me Sonny."

Later, the professor called the name of a student who was then unknown to all the jocks: "Mr. James Floyd Spikes." Mr. Spikes spoke up and said, "Sir, my nickname is Slimey, but just for this class, you can call me Slime!"

The whole class exploded with laughter, and Slimey Spikes immediately became friends with half the football team for his brilliant response under pressure.

Slimey and Cool Head signed up for the trip as did Johnny Cowart, a glad-hander from Jacksonville, Florida, as well as a couple of the married players, Fran Collins and Rusty Ninus. Seems like married guys were always in need of money. Fathom that.

The plan was to leave Troy on Friday afternoon around 5:00 p.m. and drive all the way to Miami with only food, fuel, and bathroom stops. We all purchased No Doz pills and other medicinal items to keep us awake for the long drive ahead. The group was to meet and be checked in at Lyncoach at 4:30 p.m. and be ready to roll at 5:00 p.m.

Upon arriving at Lyncoach that Friday afternoon, I had never in my life seen as many misfits and derelicts as had been assembled by Bob Sanders to drive these trucks. Some of these winos looked like they had just gotten out of jail—and probably had. There were old, young, blacks, whites, Mexicans, Asians, Indians and, I swear, a Muslim or two just to balance things off. You would have thought that a pirate ship had landed in Troy and been pillaged by this group of scallywags who were escaping down to Miami in the Ryder trucks. It would not have surprised me if a guy had shown up in a KKK outfit. I am absolutely sure that Bob used the "fog up the mirror" test to hire these characters. That is, you hold a mirror in front of someone's nose, and if he fogs up the mirror with his breath, he's hired!

Bob called us all together and announced that we were going to be separated into two groups of fifteen trucks. The first group would leave at 5:00 p.m., and the next group would leave thirty minutes later. He then introduced the "trail boss" whom we immediately dubbed "Seth Adams" (of "Wagon Train" fame). "Wagon Train" was a TV show from the '60s that featured wagon trains going west led by—you guessed it: Seth Adams.

Now Seth, like all cowboy stars, had a sidekick whose name was "Flint McCullough." Our Seth Adams also had a sidekick mechanic that we, of course, dubbed as "Flint!" Seth and Flint rode from wagon to wagon in the TV series, urging a driver to go faster or to slow down. Like them, our Seth and Flint, equipped with a sleek new Ford F-150 pickup truck with a shiny new camper on the back, were relentless in darting in and out of the caravan of southbound yellow Ryder trucks on their mission to get these trucks delivered to Miami—on time and accident free. Famous last wishes!

Leaving in two stages was a smart thing to do. Can you imagine coming up on thirty trucks that you need to pass on a two-lane road? Even though the strategy was sound, by the time we got to Florida all the trucks were back together, but by then, we were on the interstate, and that eased the problem somewhat.

As "wagon ho" (departing time) time got near, we had our trucks ready to embrace any challenges that could present themselves on the road (you know, like Indian attacks and such, and I don't mean from the outside necessarily). I couldn't speak for the other twenty-three loosely assorted pilgrims, but Slimey, Cool Head, Rusty, Fran, Johnny, and me were ready. When Seth and Flint were ready, it was Wagon Ho! Let's Go!

The route was down US Highway 231 to Dothan then on I-10 below Dothan, then over to I-75 South through the Everglades, and on to Miami.

The first incident occurred when we stopped for fuel for the first time just about an hour after we crossed the Florida state line. Everything went well with the fueling process, and all of the trucks in our division got in and back out on the interstate on schedule. I was driving the next to the last truck in the caravan, and Cool Head was the truck in front of me. As we pulled back out on the interstate from fueling up, I noticed some type of smoke coming from underneath Cool Head's truck. As we increased our speed entering the interstate, the smoke began to get heavier and was now boiling out from under the truck. Then, flames began to burst out from under the truck!

My first thought was to pull up to Cool Head's truck and get him out of it before it blew up and took Cool Head in the process. I gunned my truck with everything it could muster and pulled up to Cool Head's truck and motioned for him to pull over. Of course, he thought I was kidding when I yelled to him that his truck was on fire. Then I began to scream, "PULL OVER, damn it, PULL OVER. Your truck's on fire!"

Finally, Cool Head looked in his rearview mirror and saw the seriousness of the matter and whipped his truck off the road. I pulled my truck over in front of his and the truck behind me with Slimey Spikes in it pulled over in front of me. The three of us were hiding in the ditch and expecting an explosion any minute, just like in the movies, when to the rescue, came the trail boss Seth Adams and his sidekick Flint.

Seth immediately jumped out of his truck and ordered me and Slimey to get our trucks as far away from the debacle as possible. To hell with saving lives, let's save the trucks! While this humanitarian effort was under way, Flint crawled up under the burning truck and patted the fire out with his grease rag. It seemed that Cool Head had forgotten to release the parking brakes on the truck before he ventured back out onto the interstate, and the grinding of the brake pads had caused the fire that was destined to kill us all!

I am absolutely sure that if Seth Adams and Flint had known of any way to get rid of us, we would have been hitchhiking back to Troy after that incident. But they didn't, and like us or hate us, we were their only chance to get those trucks to Miami.

After all the smoke had cleared (literally), we were ready to get back on the trail to Miami. Just before we headed out, Seth Adams told Cool Head, who would now be leading this shortened version of the caravan, that we would be stopping for something to eat at Exit #119 and to be sure *not* to miss the exit. Cool Head assured Seth Adams we would be on top of getting off at that exit. And once again we headed out, but the other trucks had gone on.

The three trucks and Seth Adams were hustling, trying to catch up with the other trucks. We were pushing pretty hard when Seth Adams came flying out of nowhere and pulled Cool Head over. I then looked to my left out across the interstate and there, parked for what seemed a mile were bumper-to-bumper Ryder Rental trucks . . . Cool Head had missed the exit!

I can remember it so clearly today . . . Seth Adams standing in the middle of that interstate, looking up at Cool Head in that Ryder truck and yelling . . . "YOU have got to be the stupidest son-of-a-bitch I have ever known in my life!" It didn't help at all that the road sign just over Seth's shoulder that said, "Next Exit 20 miles."

Things weren't going well for Cool Head and our other two trucks. We had to drive the twenty miles down the interstate and then back twenty miles to get in on the last of a shortened supper break for us. I'm surprised that Seth let us eat at all. All trucks were now in line and ready to head down the highway to Miamiville.

During this leg of the trip, some of the "questionable" drivers began to get tired and a couple of rear-end collisions occurred. Nothing major, but a couple of the trucks were disabled and had to be towed to a local garage for repairs. Still, the caravan continued southbound to glory land. It was now well past dark. Boredom was rampant, and the No-Doze were being "popped" like candy. We were now going through the orange groves of South Central Florida, and those oranges sure looked inviting.

Just before daylight, we had our first serious wreck when an old wino, in the middle of a nap, it seems, took the backside off of one of the trucks in front of him. No one was killed, but the old guy was bruised and beat up pretty good. This wreck caused a lengthy delay—just enough time for us to raid the orange groves. I picked about a bushel of oranges, using my shirt as a bag and making several trips back to the truck to empty my bounty. All good things have to come to an end, and so it was with our orange grove raid as our slow-moving caravan began the process of carving our way through the mist of the early morning South Florida orange groves and southward once again.

As daylight came and went, I began to get very tired and sleepy. The No-Doze wasn't working, and I was slapping myself and doing everything I could to stay awake and keep that truck on the road. Then it occurred to me that the oranges might provide a possible cure for the sleepiness. I peeled a couple of the oranges and squeezed the juice into my hand then rubbed the juice into my eyes. It worked. It blinded me for a couple of miles and stung like hell, but it worked! And again, down the road we went.

As we got near our North Miami destination, no one had directions. We were just told, "Follow the truck in front of you, and you will be fine." That would have been fine if not for such things as red lights and heavy traffic. What should have been a simple "drop-off and head back home" maneuver turned into a cluster. At one point, we had all twenty-seven yellow Ryder Rental trucks lost in North Miami, Florida. I was hopelessly trying to figure out what to do, when I looked into the rearview mirror and saw five trucks following me! Seeing this, I stopped my truck and walked back to talk to Cool Head and the other drivers. We had just passed through an intersection where we saw one Ryder truck going east and another one going west! We had Ryder trucks going in every geographic direction in that town.

About the time we were about to re-board our ships and sail further into the Bermuda Triangle, a Miami police car roared up with its lights flashing. The police officer who stepped out was not happy with our little band of merry men from Troy. He instructed us to get back into our trucks and sit there until he or another police officer came back to get us. With no directions, none of the drivers knew what to do, so the Miami Police had to track each truck down and escort it to its destination.

Finally, all of the trucks were found and "brought to justice" at the Miami Ryder Truck Company. We were exhausted and began looking around for the bus that was to take us back to Troy. When no bus was found, we asked Seth Adams and Flint to point us toward the vehicle that would transport us back to Troy. They both kind of grinned and said,

"Your transportation is right over there, boys," referring to an old Merita Bread truck. We couldn't believe it! We had driven all this way, only to be loaded into the back of an old bread truck with no windows and straw on the floor. Not to mention the close association with all our misfit buddies who stunk to high heaven before we left on the trip. Man! Were we pissed!

Pissed or not, it was what it was and if we were going to get back to Troy anytime soon, we had to load up, and we did.

On the way back, we stopped at a truck stop to get our allotted meal, and you can probably imagine what we looked and smelled like. Plus, the band of derelicts that we were traveling with didn't help our credibility at all. The college boys, Cool Head, Slimey, Johnny, Fran, Rusty, and I, got a table together. As the waitress, who was cuter than your average truck stop waitress, was taking our orders, Cool Head said, "Honey, would you believe it if I told you that everybody at this table is a college student?"

The waitress stepped back, looked us all over, then looked around the room at all of our cohorts, and said, "You have got to be shitting me!" And laughing hard on the way to place our orders said, "College students? . . . Yeah, right!"

We all looked at each other and began to laugh uncontrollably; we looked like anything in the world except college kids. We were greasy, tired, and still not home.

When we finally got home, I think we all slept for two days. The day I woke up, Cool Head, Slimey, and I beat it out to Lyncoach to get paid. After taxes, we netted $198.52. Big-time cash for big-time professional drivers! At least they didn't charge Cool Head for the brakes he burned up.

CHAPTER SIX

San Francisco, by this time, was dead in our sites. The approach along I-80 was gorgeous, and the sites of the city by the bay were very picturesque. Of course, the ladies wanted to stop every mile or so and take pictures, and there was a good reason why. But good judgment prevailed, and I pushed them back into the car so we could actually visit the city, instead of sitting on a hill looking down at it.

Our first stop was Fisherman's Wharf and the famous Ghirardelli Chocolate Factory. Imagine that . . . women wanting to visit a chocolate factory! Then we had to do the bay cruise and hear all about the magnificent engineering feat of building the Golden Gate Bridge and the main attraction, Alcatraz, and all its famous long-term guests.

That evening, Lindy and I got a cheap hotel room in downtown, and Jenna and Bryna stayed with relatives. The next morning, we hit the road south down Highway One through Santa Cruz, the Monterey Peninsula, then to Carmel by the sea. We did detour in Carmel to see if Mayor Clint Eastwood had time to visit with us, but he didn't, So we went on a drive that may be the prettiest seventeen-mile stretch in the world. The roads snaked through huge redwoods and gorgeous views of the Pacific Ocean and the stunning Monterey Peninsula. We drove through and by Pebble Beach, Spyglass Hill, and Cypress Point, all world-class golf courses.

A short distance below Carmel, we stopped to take pictures of the Pacific, with its huge waves crashing down on and unmercifully pounding the rugged coastline of Northern California. I also needed to fulfill a promise for one of my girlfriends in Atlanta. Allison Wilson had bought me a bottle of champagne before I left Atlanta and asked that I open it when I got to the Pacific Ocean and think about her back in Atlanta. So to fulfill my promise, I dug through all of my junk in the Green Pig and found the bottle of champagne. The only problem was that the bottle had gotten too cold in the trunk (probably in Colorado) and exploded. Luckily, we had another bottle, but we did make a picture of me with the broken bottle and sent it back to her in Atlanta with a note that said, "The Green Pig and I made it to the Pacific, but your champagne didn't do as well! But I did think about you when we drank the substitute."

My favorite photograph was of me standing by the Green Pig with the Pacific Ocean in the background, a photo we titled, "The Pig Makes It to the Pacific." The photo was sent to any doubters of the majestic iron steed. "Ye of little faith shall learn to trust the Green Pig!"

As we loaded back into the Pig after our photo shoot and headed south down Highway One, the ladies were almost distraught from not hearing one of my stories for the past couple of days. Hell, I couldn't let them suffer anymore! So I told them about my days at Georgia College in Milledgeville—some of the best in my college career.

One of the first things that I noticed about most of the guys attending Georgia College is that they were different. In other words, most of their bubbles weren't on dead center. Most of them were the real deal, but some of them just didn't get it! One of those types was a guy named Charly Steele who thought he was a bad ass . . .The problem with his "stinking thinking" was that he had never met, seen, or had any dealings with a REAL BAD ASS. Unfortunately for Charly, that was about to change.

THE MAN OF STEELE

The eggs didn't seem to have much taste to Charly Steele as he gulped down the last morsel of what was once an appealing breakfast. The orange juice wasn't fresh, and the milk was too damn warm. The lack of talent of the lunchroom cooks was suddenly being subjected to the wrath of the "Man of Steele" on the Georgia College campus in the winter of 1967.

Charly Steele was "the big man" on campus, standing about 6 feet, 2 inches tall and weighing 225 pounds. A guy that size is fairly common on larger campuses, but at Georgia College in Milledgeville, Georgia, in 1967, there were only about 300 to 400 males enrolled (and most of them were married) versus 2,200 girls. So Charly was easily the big man on campus.

Charly's girlfriend was Cathey Ganand from Atlanta, a worldly type who had summered in Cape Cod. It was rumored that Cathey "hobnobbed" with the Kennedys. Cathey seemed to know the ways of the world in ways that Charly didn't understand. She also had varied taste in men. To her, Charly was a single coin in the big fountain. But to Charly, Cathey was the fountain—bubbly water, coins, and all!

The main reason Charly's eggs didn't taste good that morning had nothing to do with the lunchroom cooks. It mainly stemmed from the rumor around the boy's dorm (Georgia College had only one men's dorm, so the rumors were pretty accurate), that Cathey had been spotted out with

Barry Rollings again. Barry was a dashing, cool operator from down around Hinesville, Georgia. Barry had shown up for the first day of class that quarter in a three-piece, pinstriped suit and tie, with a gold watch and gold chain pinned to his vest, wearing rubber flip flops! Need I say more?

The rumors of Cathey and Barry being seen together were the work of two of Charly's stool pigeon buddies, Jimmy John Ford and Scotty Whitmire. They had promised The Man of Steele that they would research the rumors and report to him their findings at breakfast that morning. Jimmy John and Scotty actually hoped that Barry, whom they didn't care for, would suffer bodily harm in a physical conflict with Charly, ignited by their information.

When the two spies arrived at breakfast that morning, the news was not good: "Not only were Barry and Cathey together, making out at the Pub last night, we are pretty sure he got it in the parking lot, before she had to be back for her 11:00 p.m. curfew."

Charly was getting hot. How could Barry make such a fool of The Man of Steele?

"Barry knows Cathey is my girl," he pounded the lunchroom table. "Where is that son of a bitch? I'm gonna kill him!"

"We've already checked that out for you, big man, we figured this might be more than you can take from those two. Barry is over in his dorm room right now, sleeping to 10:00 a.m. like his lazy ass usually does. You ought to go over there right now and jerk his ass out of bed and beat the living shit out of him. It should be a good time to whip him because he's probably weak from screwing your girlfriend last night! We're behind you, let's get him," urged Jimmy John and Scotty, as they privately grinned and giggled at each other, when Charly wasn't looking.

With the assurances of "tweedle dumb" and "tweedle stupid," The Man of Steele was ready for action.

Charly jumped up from the breakfast table, followed by Jimmy John, Scotty, and several other student bystanders who had become interested in this unfolding saga. Charly was now roaring across campus, followed by his little band of merry men, ready to do battle with his nemesis.

Nothing much ever happened on this little campus, but plenty was about to happen! The Man of Steele led his band of supporters across campus to the lone men's dorm, then up the stairs to Barry's second-story dorm room. Still being egged on by his posse, Charly paused for a minute outside Barry's dorm room door to make sure everyone was ready. He then kicked Barry's room door open and strode over to Barry's bed with cocked fists of steel already balled up for battle.

"Ah, the coward is already covering himself with his sheets and pillows. I will put an end to his sweet dreams," Charly thought. He then snatched both the sheets and pillow covers off of Barry's bed in one move and busted him square in the kisser with one of his fists of steel! Immediately, blood spurted from Barry's lips.

It was then and there that Charly's problems truly began. In a flash of a second, he realized his mistake, but it was too late! He had not busted Barry in the mouth as he had intended. He had busted the lip of Memphis State's All-American bad-ass fullback who was Barry's best friend and was sleeping in Barry's bed as a stopover on his way home to get married that weekend!

Charly was in deep shit! The big fullback came out of that bed and ripped into Charly like he was attacking a blitzing linebacker. The self-anointed "Man of Steele" suddenly became a paper mache–punching dummy. The big man on campus was about to be brought back to reality. The big fullback, naturally stunned at first, leapt out of bed and began to beat Charly's ass with a vengeance.

Jimmy John and Scotty saw what was taking place and ran down the hall and out of the building. Charly would have been right behind them if he could, but he was busy at that moment, trying to stay alive!

The big fullback beat Charly all around the dorm room. Charly then tried to escape to the bathroom—only to have his head stuck in the toilet and flushed a couple of times, then beaten against the toilet stool. He was then dragged down the hall and kicked down the steps . . . yes, both flights.

Charly lived through it, but just barely. A week later, he was seen during finals with a head the size of a basketball and was almost unrecognizable as a human being.

And where was Barry as all of this was going on? He was sleeping in the bed across the room and woke up just in time to have a front row seat to the ass-whipping that was intended for him.

The big fullback still got married that weekend, although he had stitches in his mouth. Barry was the best man, and Cathey was also in attendance.

Charly didn't return to school after that quarter, probably fearing that the big fullback could visit Barry again, even though Jimmy John and Scotty had promised they wouldn't run a second time.

THE WABBIT AND THE WAGON

Some of the cooler guys on campus at Georgia College held a little meeting at the Student Center in the spring of 1967. Big Sid Oakley agreed with Bobby Brown, who agreed with Bill Massee, who agreed with Dodo Hollis, who agreed with Jimmy John Ford, who agreed with Bobby Barrantine, who agreed with David Dyer, who agreed with Stevie Steverson, who agreed with me, that the few, cool guys on the campus of Georgia College (there were only 300 to 400 males enrolled at that time, and most of them were married) should all secure a horse- or mule-driven buggy or wagon to escort their dates to the spring formal coming up next month. It would be BIG! And God knows this tiny college tucked away in Milledgeville, Georgia, needed something big every once in a while.

At that time, Georgia College did not have fraternities and sororities, so the spring formal was the social event of the year. Not only did Georgia College not have a formal Greek organization, some of our buddies didn't know what they were or what their function was.

One weekend, "Punk" Roberts, one of our high school buddies who opted for military service instead of college, was home on leave from the army. We fixed him up with a college girl. Punk was a little nervous and didn't talk much at first, but as he listened in on several conversations about what was happening on campuses around the country. After a couple of beers, he felt like he was catching on to the college lingo. Feeling more confident, "Punk" was ready for his first bold move of the night. He walked over and smoothly slid his arm around his date's shoulders and said, "Well, tell me, dahling, what fraternity are you in?"

After hearing that comment, Punk's date looked at him like he was a creature from Mars. A little later, she suddenly came down with a strange illness and had to be taken back to the dorm for observation.

The dress code for the dance called for formal tuxedos and gowns and, of course, upscale transportation was a must. Even though it seemed like a great idea, finding a suitable wagon, a horse or mule trained to pull it, and most important, a driver with the sense and patience to not only drive the wagon but to put up with all the hoopla that this first-ever, staged event would cause, was indeed a little daunting.

Like most well-intentioned projects of college kids, this one was put on the back burner, well, by everyone except Stevie and me. Being entrepreneurial minded guys, we struck a deal with Mr. Harold McCluney, head of the Georgia College's security force of one. Mr. McCluney had a suitable wagon and a young "green" mule that had some experience pulling wagons that "may or may not be appropriate" for this potential fiasco.

"If you boys think he will work, you can use both the wagon and mule, free of charge," offered Mr. McCluney.

When the word "free" came out of Mr. McCluney's mouth, the deal was done! Any danger of using a "green" mule was immediately abated by the word "free." Stevie and I jumped at this opportunity and made plans to have the mule and wagon delivered to the front of the Student Center on the day of the dance. Plans were made to get the green wagon with red wheels decked out with leather chairs—two in the front and two in the back—for the two distinguished, formally attired couples. A pit crew, headed by Jimmy John Ford and Jackie Whitmire, would be responsible for getting the nattily attired couples loaded and unloaded at the various stops at the women's dorms and the arrival and departure at the dance. The plan was well laid-out and solid. Stevie and I would be ready to pick up our dates in style for the Georgia College Spring Formal, 1967.

As the big weekend arrived, everything was already in place, including hiring "Rabbit," the school janitor, as the experienced wagon driver. The driver was essential to make the trip both successful and safe.

Then Stevie made a serious mistake. On the Friday afternoon of the dance, as Rabbit was getting off work at the college at 4:00 p.m., Stevie spotted him a half pint of Evan Williams "sto' bought" Whiskey, as an advance on his fee of twenty dollars for being the trusted driver of the one-vehicle wagon train. At the agreed upon meeting time and place of 5:00 p.m., at the Student Center, Rabbit was a no show!

There is no telling where that half pint of Evan Williams led Rabbit, but one thing was certain, when it was one hour away from "wagon ho" time, Rabbit was nowhere to be found. Stevie and I had just arrived back from Macon where we had gone to fetch our red paisley tuxedos, complete with top hats and canes, big cigars, plenty of red whiskey and our dates' corsages when we got the news that Rabbit was missing in action.

"Holy shit, Gary, what in the hell are we going to do? There ain't anybody we can get at this hour. I'm going to kill that fucking Rabbit come Monday, provided he shows up for work, which he probably won't," vented Stevie!

"Wait a minute, Steverson." I said, "Before you commit homicide—not that Rabbit doesn't deserve it—I may have a shot at somebody who could be available, for the right price of course."

I placed a call to my derelict buddy Lex Sellers, better known around town as "Wex Wabbit." Wex was like many of the male students who were enrolled at Georgia College at that time. Most had either flunked out, been kicked out, or were off at college somewhere else and just got homesick for Milledgeville. Lex was no different. His moniker, Wex Wabbit, came from pronouncing all of his r's like w's. He used to exclaim after a couple of drinks, "My name is Wex Wabbit, and I thow wocks at wabbits in the woad."

I anxiously dialed Wex's number. He immediately answered the phone and said, "You are in twouble, ain't you?"

"Yeah," I admitted, "how did you know?"

"Doesn't matter how I found out, I just did," said The Wabbit. "I'm already planning on skipping work out at the state hospital tonight to bail you and Steverson's ass out. I will be there shortly. Don't weave without me! Ha Ha!"

When The Wabbit showed up, he was a spectacle to behold. He whipped into the parking lot in his super-powered, modified '62 Chevy Chevelle, sporting a "bored and stroked bad-ass" 396 Chevy engine under the hood that sounded like a train coming down the street. And did I say "modified"? It seems Wex wanted a car with a little different touch than all the others around campus, so not only was his car's engine souped up, he had two commode seats installed in the back seat area. Yep, you heard right! Wex used to state, "If you wide with me, you will have the shit scared out of you, so you may as well be pwepared!"

As Wex exited his chariot, he was dressed exactly like Rabbit, the missing school janitor. He was sporting a pair of overalls, a floppy black hat, and an overcoat. Plus, he had painted his face, hands, and neck black to match the original Rabbit. This Wabbit had twuly wepwaced that Rabbit!

Now the question to be pondered, as time was running out for us to leave and pick up the girls, was, "Can Wex actually dwive this wig? Shit, I mean drive this rig?"

When questioned about his experience for being the driver of such a rig, Wex answered, "Appawently, you didn't notice what I dwove up in. This wittle ole mule and wagon ain't shit. Besides, I watch TV more than I go to class, and Wagon Twain is one of my favorites. I am well-schooled on mules and wagons. Let's go!"

And go we did! Wex popped the green mule on the butt with the reins, just like they did on Wagon Train and we were underway. Now try to picture this: You are from a South Georgia town—let's say Dublin, Georgia. You are on your way through Milledgeville on Highway 441 as it snakes its way through downtown (this was before the bypass was installed, and all out-of-town travelers formerly had to come through the middle of downtown and through Georgia College's campus). As you make the turn at Montgomery and Wilkinson Street, you meet a mule and wagon driven by a half-drunk, fake black person hauling two college kids with red paisley tuxedos on their way to the dance. Would you believe your eyes?

The first stop was to pick up my date, a lovely, well-endowed young lady from Atlanta named Ann Phillips. Ann, though forewarned, still didn't believe she would be escorted in a mule and wagon to attend the biggest social event of the year. As the mule and wagon trekked through campus and pulled up in front of Atkinson Hall, a crowd had already gathered. Then, with timing similar to a NASCAR pit crew, Jimmy John and Jackie's crew, showed up with portable steps. They ran out and placed the steps against the wagon so that the dignitaries could alight and escort to the wagon Miss Ann Phillips, a stunned young lady who had never seen anything quite like this in her life! Here was her date, sporting a red paisley tux, top hat, cane, and cigar. He was holding her corsage and, with his little entourage, was waiting to board pretty Miss Ann to be escorted to the dance.

By this time, the dorm had almost emptied. Camera flashbulbs were popping, and even girls who didn't have dates wanted to come out and be a part of this spectacle.

Then, we were off to pick up Stevie's date, the lovely Miss Brenda Boatwright of Statesboro, Georgia. Stevie was in over his head on this one, but Brenda kept going out with him because of popular stunts (similar to the mule and wagon) and the notoriety it gave her.

As the crew was headed to pick up Brenda across campus and down Clark Street, almost exactly in front of the governor's mansion, the worst possible thing happened. The entourage was pulled over by the cops! Not just any cops. It was the infamous pair of defenders of Justice, Niblet and Wolf, two no-nonsense cops who had the reputation of spoiling many a high school or college kid's night on the town. They would write tickets or haul desperados off to jail or, even worse, phone their parents.

With the police car's lights flashing, Niblet and Wolf approached the mule and wagon, sort of just looked around and said the unthinkable: "You guys must be crazy to think you could pull off a stunt like this without offering ole Niblet and Wolf a ride! This rig is too cool for you guys. Who came up with this idea for y'all? Now, get your asses on down the road, and have a good time."

Not only did they not arrest the motley crew, they stopped us three or four more times that night to see if we would change our minds and let them ride in the wagon with us.

As the traveling sideshow pulled up in front of Brenda's dorm, the news had spread across campus of what was coming. Again, the dorm almost emptied to see the show. And Miss Brenda Boatwright, like her counterpart Miss Phillips, was shocked at what a spectacle she would be joining. Again, flash bulbs were popping, and again, there was

Jimmy John and Jackie with their crew to escort Miss Brenda into the wagon.

The question now was, "Could the little green mule pull the wagon around the hilly campus with a full load and an inexperienced driver?"

Upon hearing the concerns of the passengers, Wex Wabbit assured everyone that if the mule couldn't make it up the hill, everyone but him could just get out and walk. Amazingly, the mule never acted like it was too much of a strain and, luckily, nobody had to walk. When the mule and wagon (and, by this time, its slightly inebriated passengers and driver) arrived at the dance, it was like the king and his court had arrived back at the castle after being away on an extended stay. Again, there was Jimmy John and his crew, albeit a little slower and less attentive because of the amount of alcohol consumed. The thought of the low pay scale he and his crew would receive didn't help, either. But they had done their job quite well and, because of this, Stevie and I gave them the rest of the night off . . . without pay, of course.

As the two couples and their esteemed carriage arrived at the dance, there was a sort of celebrity aura about it—not about being famous (though maybe we were that night), but being the guys who pulled off a truly unique southern college experience. This magical experience would be talked about around Georgia College and Milledgeville, Georgia, for a long time.

Everyone at the dance wanted to have their picture taken in the mule and wagon. The photographer who had set up a fake waterfall and pond inside the dance, had to move outside and set up by the mule and wagon to get any sustained business. Think about it. Would you want a picture of you and your date next a fake waterfall, when you could have it made next to a fake black guy, in a green wagon with red wheels?

"What a unique college town story. It seems like the whole school and the city was behind your effort to make something happen at ole Georgia College. I'll bet people in Milledgeville are still talking about that one," said Jenna.

"The question I have is, "What in the hell did y'all come up with to top that effort?" asked Bryna.

"Believe it or not, Steve came up with a sequel the following year that by all expectations should have topped the Mule and Wagon stunt, but the Mule and Wagon's bar was set pretty high," I added.

Find out for yourself how the two Georgia College/Milledgeville extravaganzas compared and how they ended up.

STEVIE WEAVIE PUTS ON THE RITZ

In the fall of 1968, during my first school year at Troy State University, I got a call from my good friend Steve Steverson. I had teamed up with Steve the year before at Georgia College to have our dates picked up and escorted to the Spring Formal in a mule and a wagon.

Steve, a consummate showman, was still in school at Georgia College and was working at the Holiday Inn as a nighttime bookkeeper. His boss, Mr. J. C. Green, had allowed Steve to work double shifts so he could have the weekend off to host a huge party he had planned at the Holiday Inn. This was the blowout party "Stevie Weavie" called me about.

Steve could hardly control his excitement as he told me about the grand affair he had planned. He said, "Spillers, you have got to come home and bring some of your roughneck buddies from Troy with you. Y'all will have a blast! I guarantee it. This is going to be bigger than the mule and wagon. I've rented the banquet room at the Holiday Inn and have sold fifty tickets already. We are going to have a coat and tie, shish kabob, and champagne dinner. Then, we are going to fly our dates in a helicopter from the Holiday Inn to the National Guard Armory where The Tams, one of the hottest college show bands of the '60s, are playing in concert that night. How does that sound big boy? Are you in?"

"Hell yes, I'm in!" I retorted.

Even though I was on a football scholarship, I was redshirted and therefore not eligible to play in games my first year at Troy. It was easy to go home if we had an away game, which we did on the weekend Steve had his throwdown planned. I invited Eddie Minor from Jacksonville, Florida, and "Jumpin" Jim Caldwell from Bay Minette, Alabama, to go along for the weekend.

When the big weekend of the party rolled around, we headed out to Milledgeville early on Friday. Most of the guests of the party were staying at the Holiday Inn, and Steve had managed to get my buddies and me a couple of comp rooms also.

This unique event was planned for Friday night. The banquet was the first thing on the agenda. Steve had gone to the expense of hiring a chef. Just before the meal was served, the lights would be dimmed. The chef was to sprint through the swinging doors of the kitchen and into the banquet room, and . . . PHOOF, light the shish kabobs in a stunning display of culinary dexterity and charm.

To really go any further with this story, you have got to realize that Milledgeville, Georgia, is no typical small southern town. The population isn't that large, but the number of interesting characters we have in that town is miraculous. You are about to meet some of them.

My date for the night was one of my best friends from high school, Nicki Spase. Nicki was the captain of our Baldwin Braves High School cheerleading squad and was currently home from the University of Georgia, visiting her parents for the weekend. We hadn't seen each other for a long time and thought this little social outing would be a fun event to attend together.

As Nicki and I pulled up to the Holiday Inn that Friday evening to attend the banquet, across the parking lot came one of my closest buddies in the world and one of the zaniest characters to ever call Milledgeville home, Wex Wabbit Sellers (AKA Lex Sellers). Wex, driver of the mule and wagon affair from a year earlier, was a good friend of Nicki's also, so we decided to walk in together.

Instead of going around the building to the banquet room entrance like anyone with any sense at all would do, we just walked through the Holiday Inn's main dining room (which was at that time where many of the "well-to-do folks" from Milledgeville commonly dined on Friday evening).

Nicki and I were dressed appropriately, but Lex's attire was something to see. He had found, and was wearing, an old brown baggy, sweat-stained Humphrey Bogart suit made in 1930s or '40s. His tie and straw hat were red, and his straw hat read "Wallace for President" (George Wallace was running for president that year). Wex's shoes were brown-and-white saddle oxfords. The suit itself was enough to draw attention, but that wasn't good enough for Wex. Halfway through the dining room tables, approximately the middle of the restaurant, a loud clanging alarm clock began ringing.

I had no idea what was happening. My first reaction was that it was a fire alarm (as did about half the people in the restaurant). Wex assured everyone not to worry. He then started pulling on a rope that went down into his oversized pants pocket and retrieved a ringing alarm clock! He shut off the alarm clock and announced to all the patrons of the dining room that it was time to take a drink—because fifteen minutes had passed since he had had one. And drink he did, straight from a bottle of Jack Daniel's that he had fetched from another baggy pocket.

After that scene, Nicki and I sprinted to the rear exit of the restaurant and over to the banquet room. Meanwhile, Wex was being escorted out of the restaurant and over to the banquet room by the restaurant manager.

When we entered the banquet room, everything looked great, that is, everything except the host, Stevie Weavie, who already seemed to be a bit shit-faced. Apparently, the loss of sleep from working doubles combined with some strong, brown drink had his head spinning early. Guests were slowly beginning to arrive, and Stevie was glad-handing with everyone and welcoming them in.

Then came this loud, weird, pulsating, sound from above the Holiday Inn, and almost immediately came the announcement that the helicopter had arrived and had landed on the front lawn of the hotel. Immediately, the small crowd rushed outside to check out the late-night transportation.

The first two "test riders" were Stevie and Wex Wabbit. Big mistake. The pilot, not realizing that he had two drunks on board until he had taken off for the test ride, circled the Holiday Inn and, within a couple of minutes, brought the two co-pilots back before they crashed the helicopter. (Apparently, both Steve and Wex Wabbit were flipping switches and generally creating a flight hazard in the cockpit.) As soon as the pilot coerced Stevie and Wex into exiting the aircraft, he took off and didn't come back!

Nicki didn't know what to think about Steve Steverson. "Is he like this all the time?" she asked.

"No, just when he is awake."

"Man, I would never want to go out with that stupid fool!"

"I don't blame you. He is kind of a wild ass, but he really is a nice guy. Not much of a helicopter co-pilot, but a nice guy anyway."

After the excitement of the helicopter pilot "blowing this gig," everyone returned to the banquet room to get the festivities started sans the helicopter rides, of course.

Steve assured everyone not to worry about getting a refund on the helicopter portion of the tickets, because he had not paid the pilot. Now the only problem was getting the money back from Stevie Weavie.

As time got ever so close to beginning the festive dinner, everyone began to take their seats and to pour themselves a drink to last them through dinner. Nicki and I were seated next to Wex Wabbit. As we took our seats, I noticed that Wex was missing, probably thrown off the property by the Holiday Inn staff by now. Why, in just less than an hour's time, he had set off what was perceived to be a fire alarm coming from his pants pocket in the main dining room and had almost crashed a helicopter on the front lawn of the Inn. What could they be upset about?

Wex's chair being empty and his presence not accounted for could be good or bad. My vote was that it was bad! We would just have to wait and see.

It was now banquet time! About twenty-five couples were in attendance. Everyone was sharply dressed and ready for dinner and whatever the rest of the evening had to offer.

Stevie Weavie, the self-appointed master of ceremonies, had seated himself at the center of the head table. When it was time to get started, Stevie, shit-faced as he was, dinged on his glass and said "Otay, Otay! I want to ast Sid Oakley to ast the blewssing."

Whereupon "Big Sid" stood up and bellowed, "Fuck the blessing! Let's eat!"

This announcement was immediately followed by a hearty round of applause and cheering. Stevie Weavie acknowledged Brother Oakley's request, sat down in his seat, fell forward and passed out, face first, into his salad plate! And yes, the salad and dressing was already in the plate.

Nicki was aghast! "What kind of animal is this person, Gary?"

"A sleepy kind, I guess," I believe was my answer.

We got Stevie's head turned so that he didn't suffocate on blue cheese dressing, while everyone else prepared for dinner to be served. It was time to dim the lights and allow the chef to present the evening's main creation. Even though nothing had gone right that evening, there was a hopeful moment, in which all had been forgiven, including errant alarm clocks and a hasty exit by the helicopter pilot. Finally, in the first stages of the meal, the chef would win everyone's heart over with his presentation of the flaming shish kabobs.

Drum roll please. Dim the lights. Here came the chef through the swinging doors of the kitchen. He burst into the middle of the banquet room when, out of nowhere, Wex Wabbit appeared and jumped on the chef's back. Wabbit was whooping and hollering like a cowboy and whipping the chef with a rolled-up cloth dinner napkin shaped like a jockey's whip. And, like the jockeys at Churchill Downs, Wex was "going to the whip" in the last quarter mile.

Everyone was amused, but this was their dinner. "Big Sid" and some of the other guys finally freed the chef from Wex, so that he could light the shish kabobs and then serve dinner to the well-entertained, but hungry guests.

After the banquet, most of the guests loaded up to go to The Tams concert at the National Guard Armory. No longer having the option of a helicopter ride, it was every man for himself in getting his date transported to the concert from the Holiday Inn. Nicki and I rode in my car, and Wex drove his souped-up Chevelle. Yeah, the one with the two toilet seats in the back in place of the rear seat.

Needless to say, Wex was not well received at the National Guard Armory with his Wallace hat and tie. The Tams was an all-black band, and Wallace was a racist from Alabama who was making some headway in his run for President of the United States. At first, there were no problems, but when Wex jumped up on the stage and tried to sing with the band, he was escorted to the door. Unlike the reprieve he got from the Holiday Inn, here he was told not to come back.

Nevertheless, The Tams put on a great show as usual, and a good time was had by all. Well, most all.

When we got back to the Holiday Inn, it looked like a war zone. People were running around half-nekkid, and two guys were dueling with the fire extinguishers. One inebriated party-goer approached Eddie Minor (who was one of my teammates at Troy and a big ole boy) close to the pool and said, "Don't mess with me, Big Boy, cause I know 'kasate'!"

Eddie says, "What's that?"

The guy responded, "That's how you fight with your feet!"

"Show me."

"I'll have to take my shoes off," said the drunk, and he did. As he began going through his gyrations to show Eddie kasate, Eddie bent over, picked up the guy's shoes, and threw them in the swimming pool. And it was a very cold fall night.

The guy looked at Eddie and said in a pitiful voice, "What did you do that for?"

Eddie responded, "Surely anybody that knows 'kasate' certainly knows how to use his feet to swim!"

The last Eddie saw of the "kasate expert" was an expert diving exhibition on behalf of the "expert" in search of his shoes in the pool.

With all the excitement going on, Stevie Weavie finally woke up from his salad plate pillow and began wandering around, trying to figure out what hit him. With all the carnage around the Inn, he was certain that he would be fired on Monday morning. As we were standing there talking, here came the local cops who were, as usual, too late to make any difference, but just in time to help get Stevie fired.

Actually, Stevie wasn't fired on Monday after all, as Mr. Green was not only a patient person but a forgiving one as well.

On Monday morning, there was a picture of the helicopter on the front lawn of the Holiday Inn in *The Union Recorder*, the local newspaper. Thank God the paper did not tell the story of why the helicopter was there and, more important, why it left so quickly.

Other interesting tidbits from that weekend included the fact that we never heard from Jim Caldwell that night after the banquet as he and his appointed date, Wanda Wilson, never left their hotel room. Jim decided he had the best-looking girl he had been with in a while (maybe forever) in bed with him. Why let her out to greet the public at his expense?

Another very interesting development took root that night. Nicki Spase, who swore after that night that she would never be seen on the face of this earth with Steve Steverson, ended up marrying that very "scallawag" two years later!

Wex Wabbit threatened to show up at Steve and Nicki's wedding in a gorilla suit, selling popcorn. Wex's promise was so sincere that Nicki, fearing the worst for her wedding party, warned the wedding planners to be on the outlook for a person dressed as a gorilla . . . selling popcorn! This gorilla would be easy to spot by the wedding guests because he would be pronouncing all of his "r's" like "w's"!

Lindy was all over the amazing turn of events that got Nicki and Steve together in marriage. "Nicki just sounds like a cool lady who could have done a lot better than Steve," she commented.

"Actually, it has worked out pretty good. Steve is a budding investment banker, and Nicki is teaching school. They live in Atlanta and seem to be very happy," I added.

CHAPTER SEVEN

The drive down California Highway One was a sharp contrast to the drive through Kansas. Instead of every recurring scene being the same and completely boring, each scene on the California coast played out as an exciting natural event. Each wave was different! Each rock cliff and sandy beach bore a new visual pleasure. Seagulls, pelicans, and various other seabirds of beauty darted from the ocean out of the clouds and shot up across the highway and up the sides of the cliffs on the roadside as we motored south. Sea lions, otters, and seals barked to us from their jagged rock fortresses out in the ocean. (Maybe they thought the Green Pig was one of them.)

Georgia's coastline could not match what we were experiencing that day, but neither could many other coastlines in the entire world. California Highway One was a true spectacle of amazing seaside beauty that left us speechless.

During a quiet time motoring south down the coastline when the girls were either snoozing or reading, my mind drifted, as it did quite often in those days, back to Cheryl and our planned meeting in Los Angeles the next day. We had kept in touch and had planned to meet somewhere on the trip, but hadn't decided on Los Angeles until a couple of days prior. Being a flight attendant, she could go on a moment's notice on her days off, and the next day I was to pick her up at LAX. We were to stay with an old friend from Milledgeville, Billy Cordoza. Billy was in the men's clothing business and had an apartment at Huntington Beach, then and now a hot spot for singles and one of the meccas of the West Coast beach scene. The girls were staying with relatives again, and Cheryl and I were scheduled to share Billy's sofa in his one-bedroom apartment.

When we arrived in Los Angeles, I dropped off the girls at their relatives and hooked up with Billy for a late-night beer. Even though I was excited to see Billy, I was much more interested in seeing Cheryl the next day. It was a long, sleepless night.

Though I was anxious to see Cheryl, things had changed. It was going to take a while to get back to where we were in our relationship. Several times over the previous month, my calls to her had not been returned—sometimes for days. She always had an excuse, but most of the time I didn't believe her. My situation hinged on believing her or calling her hand. For the present time, I chose to make her think I believed her, the obvious cowardly way out.

Going to LAX in the Green Pig was quite an experience. Cheryl was to meet me outside baggage claim, but she didn't know what the Pig looked like. I was still driving my red Mercedes when I had last seen her. As I pulled up to baggage claim, she was standing there with her hand shading her eyes, looking all around for any vehicle that would resemble a Green Pig among all the Mercedes, BMWs and Porsches. Cheryl was not the superficial type and laughed out loud when she finally recognized me and the Pig. She bolted over to the car, threw her travel bag in the back, and jumped in, "How's my Dog doing?" (She had given me this nickname from the way I acted when I got inebriated.) She followed up her grand entrance with a very passionate kiss. GOD! I had missed this woman!

On the way back to Billy's, it was mid-morning, and we were trying to catch up with each other and talk about the plans for the next couple of days, which included visits to Hollywood, Universal Studios, the beaches and a trip the next day down to San Diego and Tijuana. Cheryl was all into sightseeing, and I was all into spending the next two days on the sofa. You know who won that battle. After getting Cheryl back to the apartment and literally ripping her clothes off, we made love for what seemed like hours (ok . . .ok . . .well maybe 15 minutes).

After a shower and change of clothes, we met my "traveling harem" and Billy for lunch in West Los Angeles at The Greenview Thai Restaurant. Of course, the girls were in search of celebrities and, thank God, none showed up that day. We visited the Grauman's Chinese Theater and checked out all the star's imprints. Then, we were off to Universal Studios for the tourist trap tours.

It was very interesting to see the actual sets of many of the shows that I had seen on TV or at the movies. Jaws had just been released that year, and the studio's reenactment of the film was realistic and fun.

The next day, we piled everyone into the Green Pig for the trip to San Diego and Tijuana. We figured that if the Mexican government seized our vehicle, the joke would be on them! The Green Pig, I am sure, didn't appreciate that assessment of its worth, but like I told a girlfriend once, "IF I had any feelings, you would have hurt them!"

The drive down the southern coast was pretty, but nothing to compare to the excitement that was generated by its northern counterpart along Highway One. We had a pleasant, late lunch in San Diego, and the scenery was beautiful until we got to Mexico.

As our licenses were checked and we entered Mexico, it was like going into a different world. Tijuana had earned its reputation as a sleazy border town with plenty of crime, corruption, and drug problems. Nothing that I saw that day changed that image . . . except the mariachi singers and players. Everywhere we went, we encountered another happy band of mariachi players who wanted to serenade us with one more song. Of course, we bought the requisite sombreros and vests to blend in, enjoyed an authentic Mexican dinner that evening, and drank world-record proportions of tequila! All I remember about heading back to the good ole USA was Billy's driving, the bright lights of all different colors at the border, and a lot of Mexicans with guns.

The next day I awoke with Cheryl in my arms, and she clung to me as if she didn't want to let go. Then, it hit me that this could be the last night we would spend together, on Billy Cordoza's sofa of all intimate places. I don't know why I felt this way, but there was a strong sentiment that I would never see her again after this trip.

Later that day, I dropped Cheryl off at LAX. Again, she would not let go of what seemed like an hour-long hug. Finally, we separated. She looked deep into my eyes as I looked deep into hers. She said, "Dog, I LOVE YOU!"

It was the first time she had ever told me that when she was sober or not just playing around. I had this weird feeling and knew then that I would never see her again. She turned with tears streaming down both cheeks to walk away and board her plane; she never looked back. If I was capable of crying, I would have. I wasn't and I didn't, but God, I loved that woman!

****

Jenna and Bryna had made travel arrangements to get back to Aspen to finish out the season. The snow season had made a serious rebound. What appeared at one time to become a disastrous year could end up with record snowfalls in the winter and spring seasons. Lindy and I and the Green Pig hit the road back toward Geor-gee.

My good friend Wilbur Bell from Bremen, Georgia, would visit me on weekends and would always wake me up in the early morning on Sunday mornings by popping the top on a beer can and tapping on the door of my bedroom and saying, "Spallers, it's time to git back to Georg-gee." This meant, by God, it was time to take him back home to Bremen because he had had all the fun he could stand in one weekend.

So Lindy and I had made the big, West Coast turnaround and were headed back to Geor-gee.

Our first stop on the trip back was Las Vegas, which was only three hours away. Neither of us had ever been there, and we were pumped to have the opportunity to visit one of the great destinations in the world.

"All of the bright lights and big city fever is okay, but what I would like for you to do is tell me a couple of your stories to get me in the mood to party," said Lindy.

So I agreed to tell her two wild, fun-oriented tales one about "Okefenokee Walph" and the other about the "Deuce and a Quarter."

"Lindy, you have had issues with my stories, complaining that my tales are male-dominated with the women getting screwed in the end. Well, I'm here to tell you that ain't the case in this little tale," I said.

OKEFENOKEE WALPH AND THE BARTENDER

It had been a hot steamy July day in Georgia's Okefenokee Swamp, a huge swamp that seems like it covers most of South Georgia. The Native American Indians called it the "land of the trembling earth." Or is that the Everglades down in Florida? Regardless of which one you are talking about, they both are huge swamps, covering several thousands of acres, and I am certain that the earth trembles under both of them quite regularly, especially when the Yankee tourists come in great numbers each summer to get a look at a real, live alligator.

It was mid-August, and Stevie Stephens and his tongue-tied buddy, Walph Watson, had been working at their summer jobs in the swamps as tour guides, serving the never-ending stream of Yankee tourists that inundate the park each year. Usually, the tourists were on their way to Florida. Their hope was to see a real live alligator in its natural habitat.

There is some type of fixation Yankees have with alligators. Walph always wondered why they couldn't just feed the obnoxious Yankee tourists to the alligators and save the state a lot of money. Stevie reminded Walph on many occasion that that would never work. "If we feed the alligators the tourists, they might quit coming back, and we would be in a helluva fix with a bunch of fat alligators and nobody to show them to."

Stevie figured if the Yankee tourists were dumb enough to pay good money to be paddled around in a boat, swatting mosquitos—and no telling what other types of insects—to search for gators and other swamp inhabitants, they had better keep a good supply of them coming back each and every year.

It was now quitting time, and both Stevie and Walph had been at it since sunrise. It was time to head home to Waycross, located just up the road a bit. But dotted along that small stretch of US Highway One between the swamp and Waycross was the lure and temptation of several choice cold beer joints, each joint had a bar with its own distinct personality built from 2 x 4's or 2 x 6's, sanded down and shellacked. There'd be sawdust on the floor, a refrigerator or two for the beer, a pool table, a TV for the afternoon soaps and football games on the weekends and, of course, a jukebox carrying the most popular country tunes from Waylon Jennings, Hank Williams, and Merle Haggard.

On this day, it was Walph's turn to buy the after-work refreshments. Of course, the one who bought said refreshments got to select the joint that was patronized that day. For some reason, Walph selected a joint a little closer to town than usual, one they had never been in before. As they pulled up, Walph reminded Stevie, "If dey are all awike, why would dis one be differunt?"

"You're buying, Bubba. Let's go," replied Stevie.

As the two, highly trained public servants of the Okefenokee Swamp passed through the screened door, they both noticed that this little oasis was just like all the rest except for one thing: the bartender. The bartender was a rather stout woman, carrying about 225 pounds of pure muscle. She had on a pair of cut-off overalls (bermuderalls, as my friend's dad used to call 'em) and displayed Olympic shot putter–type legs. Her arms had the standard tattoos of Mom, a naked woman, and 13 & 1/2 (which stands for 1 for the judge, 12 for the jury, and a half-ass chance of getting out!). Her hair was pulled back in a ponytail, which gave her an austere, manly look. If she had smiled (which she didn't), she would have revealed that her two front teeth were missing. (The story was she'd had a fight with a pulpwooder after he got drunk and made a pass at her girlfriend. It was rumored afterward that the pulpwooder talked in a much higher tone of voice and had no reason to ask *any* girl to dance, especially the bartender's friend.)

Walph was excited to be in the new place and took charge immediately by blurting out, "Otay baby, give me and ole Stevie hewer two weely cold smudweisers and some of dem weely good-smewlling woasted peanuts over thar."

The stout bartender gave Walph an intimidation stare that even Hulk Hogan couldn't possibly conjure up any better for his Saturday night *wrestlin' match* with the Undertaker. Saying not a word to anybody, the bartender went to the refrigerator and fetched two longneck bottles of Budweiser, walked over to the bar in front of Walph and Stevie, then reached across the bar and busted the first bottle of beer over Walph's head. Walph immediately went to his knees from the force of the blow. She then took the other bottle and busted it over his head, knocking Walph cold as a cucumber!

The bartender then turned to Stevie, grabbed him by the collar, brushed back her ponytail, and said, "Slook here buddy, swhen that mulla fuckner wakes up, yous tell him he had better snot ever come in shere and mock me ever again."

"Now," she said as she released Stevie's collar, "Would you slike a beer and some woasted peanuts? The first two were on me."

"What a coincidence. Who would have thought that both Walph and the bartender would be hairlipped?" said Lindy.

"Walph for one," I said. "I will bet you that Walph won't be darkening the door of that joint anymore . . . even if 'they are all awike'."

The next tale is about an interrupted hunting trip delayed by my brother, Larry, and his buddy Barney Beall.

DEUCE AND A QUARTER

It was the fall of 1972 in Milledgeville, Georgia, during deer season. One evening around 7:00 p.m., two friends, Tom Hines and Jack Maddox, and I were playing cards over at my trailer at Townsend's Trailer Park. We were basically killing time before heading up to our deer camp to spend the night and get ready for an early-morning hunt.

"The moon looks good out there tonight . . . as bright as it is now should make it a good morning to hunt the big racks!" Tom stated.

"Big racks, small racks, or medium, if one walks by me in the morning I'm gonna put an end to his day early. I need some meat in the freezer," I offered.

"Shit, ain't neither one of you gonna come close to the hoss I'm going to take down in the morning," bragged Jack. As usual, the banter had begun before the hunt, about who would kill the biggest buck or who truly was the world's greatest outdoorsman. It was about this time that the side door of my trailer (this was before trailers were called "manufactured homes") flew open and there they stood, arm in arm with each other: my brother, Larry, and his best buddy, Barney Beall. And, as they say in the South, they were "tore up" (intoxicated beyond normal human limits). They were truly best friends, but that night they were closer than ever! They kept saying to us, "Dis is my bess friend and if anybody fucks wiff my friend, I will kill their ass! DO you understand me?"

I still don't know how they were able to drive a vehicle to my place but, miraculously, they did. Larry and Barney began bugging me about something to drink, and they weren't talking about any sissy-ass beer either. They wanted a man's drink. "Come on Gary, you got some good stuff hid out around here and we know it, so come on we need a drink," begged Barney.

I then remembered that I did have something stored away that might be just what they needed to knock them out so we could go to the deer camp and not worry about them driving home.

"Guys," I announced, "I do truly have a man's drink that both of you will enjoy." Just in the past week, some of my buddies from Troy had been in town and wanted some good ole southern moonshine, so I'd gone over to Evaleena's (my father's favorite moonshiner) and picked up a quart of her Sunday best. I still had most of it because after two shots each, my buddies from Troy had to be let out of the car in downtown Milledgeville so they could puke on and make love to most every tree on the campus of Georgia Military College. It was a helluva sight!

I got the moonshine out from under the sink and poured both Barney and Larry a shot while reading to them the mandatory warning listed just under the skull and crossbones on the jar: "Drink at your own risk; it may be your last."

After the shots were downed, Tom, Jack, and I waited around to see what would happen . . . nothing. Absolutely nothing. I think the shots may have calmed them down a bit, but this presented another problem. Even though the moonshine hadn't knocked them out, they certainly were not any more sober or in any shape to drive. Not only that, Barney had become almost incoherent and could not tell us where he lived. Though not much better than Barney, through mumbling and hand signals, Larry persuaded us that he knew where Barney lived.

We loaded Barney and Larry in the back; Jack and I got in the front. Oh, did I mention the vehicle that I was driving that evening—a brand new Oldsmobile 225—belonged to my girlfriend's father? Julie Clark was a well-to-do blonde bombshell from Jacksonville, Florida, whose father owned a truck trailer company. I had volunteered to drive Julie's car while mine was being worked on. She had been parking the car at my place because she didn't have the proper campus stickers. I was temporarily driving Mr. Clark's car while mine was in the shop.

So, we motored across town to take Barney home. The plan was to dump Barney, then take Larry back to the trailer to sleep it off after calling Angela, Larry's wife, to tell her about their predicament. We thought Barney lived on the north side of town just off Jefferson Street, so we headed that way. When we thought we were there, Barney was snoozing. But on cue, Larry started waving and pointing, so we pulled into the driveway and began reviving Barney. Barney sat up in the seat and peered at the house, then blinked his eyes and looked at us without saying a word. I asked Barney if that was his house. Barney looked again at the house, then back at us and said, "I ain't never seen this goddamn place before in my life!"

So off we went, again, still traveling north. We turned east onto Ivey Station Road. Barney's mumbling and Larry's gyrations made us think we were close. But for some reason, I thought we were going the wrong way, so I turned around and headed west on Ivey Station. The turning around, the backing up, and taking off again must have woken up Barney. He sat up in his seat and started looking around. Jack yelled at him and asked, "Barney, is this the right road?"

Barney, after thinking about the question replied, "You are on the right road, but you are going backwards!" Meaning of course, we were on the right road, just going the wrong way. So again, we did the all too-familiar turning around process. But it wasn't your typical turnaround in the road scenario this time. As soon as I got the car turned around yet again . . . here came the smell emanating from the back seat . . . moonshine! Larry was throwing up on Barney or vice-versa. It really didn't matter. It was a mess and in the backseat of my girlfriend's father's new car. Shit, I was going to be disowned before we ever went steady. As soon as I smelled the hideous slime, I whipped the car over to the side of the road, slammed to a stop, ran around, and jerked the door open. When I did, Larry rolled past me into the ditch followed by Barney, both puking, but faithfully hanging on to each other.

Picture this if you can, or if you care to: Here we were, sitting on the side of the road at about 8:30 p.m., with all four doors open on the car. Larry was all the way in the ditch; Barney was halfway up the bank of the ditch, a death grip on Larry with one hand and a death grip on the car with the other hand. Both of them were puking, with Tom, Jack, and me looking on in amazement.

"What in the hell are we going to do?" asked Jack and Tom.

I answered, "We gotta get their asses out of that ditch and back into that car, smell or no smell. I'll take care of the car tomorrow.

"Okay," said Jack, "let's go boys." As he reached down to pull Larry out first, he grabbed his arm, but his grip slid off because of the slime on Larry's arm. Then Jack started throwing up, too.

"Holy shit," I said and jumped down in the ditch to help Jack. Then, the smell hit me and I started throwing up, too. So there we were, with two drunks still in the ditch and two sober guys trying to get them out, all puking their guts out. If it hadn't been for Tom's strong stomach, we might never had gotten out of there that night.

After some extreme effort, we got everyone loaded into my future ex-father-in-law's car (before he was even my father-in-law). We then headed down the road to Barney's house. Both Larry and Barney, who were somewhat lucid by this time, were able to get us to Barney's house . . . FINALLY!

But trouble was brewing there also. As we pulled into Barney's driveway, we looked up toward the house. Standing in the picture window of the house with her arms folded and resembling Mr. Clean was Barney's rather large wife, Mary Jean. Barney looked at me and said, "Uh-oh!"

Sitting there with two shirt pockets full of puke, Barney again looked up at Mary Jean then back at me and said, "You got any chewing gum?"

As Barney got out of the car, he must have crossed the driveway three times before he made it to the house. When he got to the house and as we were driving off, Mary Jane had turned the water hose on Barney and made him strip down and take his clothes straight to the laundry room.

We finally made it to the hunting camp, but it was a little later than usual! No one killed a deer the next morning. I think it could have been the smell.

CHAPTER EIGHT

Lindy and I were excited about our stayover in Las Vegas. What she was not excited about was that I might want to start gambling again. She laid down the law: if I started gambling, I was NOT to come to her for money if I got behind and lost my money.

I had a grand total of twenty-eight dollars in my pocket at the time. I anticipated that we would be able to spend the night, have a couple of drinks, and hit the road early the next morning. I would have to stop somewhere soon and ask my family to wire me money to get me the rest of the way home. Lindy, bless her Midwestern upbringing, was a very frugal young lady and was never one to pay for a tab or offer to buy dinner or, God forbid, make a small loan.

Everything was, as we agreed, fifty-fifty, and she held me to that.

We got a room at the Stardust Hotel and Casino for a give-away price of eighteen dollars per night. We showered and got ready to go out for a complimentary cocktail and a sandwich in the casino. As we were walking around in the Casino trying to pirate some food and drink, I stopped at a blackjack table and made a minimum two-dollar bet and won. So I reloaded and won again, and again, and again. After watching for what turned out to be a couple of hours, Lindy left in disgust and went back to the room.

I kept playing, and my fortune was rising. At one time, I had 700 dollars in poker chips in front of me, and I was still winning. Everything was going very well when these huge black guys approached our table. One of them looked familiar, and he should have. It was Mohammed Ali in his prime. Apparently, he and his friend knew the dealer at our table, and they were bantering with him when I noticed Mohammed Ali's outfit. He was wearing a denim coat and matching jeans. When he turned away, I saw that he had a switch stitched into the back of the coat across the shoulder blade area. Under the switch was stitched "Bear Hunting," referring to the old adage that it takes a pretty bad mother to go bear hunting with a switch . . . at that time in his career, Mohammed Ali qualified!

As my fortune mounted, my memory fogged up and the next twenty-four to forty-eight hours became a blur. I woke up in the Green Pig in the parking lot of Caesars Palace Hotel with my stylish, plaid seersucker suit still on me. All my money was gone, and I had no idea where I had been the last day or two. That was the first and last time something like that has happened to me. But at that moment, there I was.

I started searching all of my pockets and found a 100-dollar poker chip from Caesars Palace in my coat. I immediately went inside and cashed it in. I was ahead of the game again. I now had more money than I showed up with and was ready to hit the road again . . . but wait! Where was Lindy?

I went back to the Stardust Hotel, and the front desk had an envelope addressed to me from Lindy. The letter said, "I don't know what happened to you, and I don't care. The last time I saw you, you were rolling in money and doing well. I kept trying to get you to quit, but you wouldn't. So I finally gave up and went back to the room. I woke up the next morning and you weren't around, so I booked a flight back to Atlanta where I am sure I will be when you read this letter. Good luck on the rest of the trip, and call me when you get back to Atlanta. Lindy"

Damn. Gone, just like that! Hell, I was getting tired of her constant bitching anyway. Where's the service station? I needed to fill up and get on the road? The ungrateful bitch!

After a quick "whore's bath" in the public bathroom of the Stardust and a fill-up with gas, I left Las Vegas and headed out on Highway 63, crossing the magnificent Hoover Dam just outside Las Vegas and then down to I-40 and back east. Anybody who says Herbert Hoover never accomplished anything as President needs to see the Hoover Dam! This magnificent engineering feat is said to hold back up to nine trillion gallons of water.

After my Las Vegas experience, my homing device was set for Geor-gee. I drove within fifty miles of the Grand Canyon and didn't stop. I also passed on several historical markers that I was truly interested in, such as where Billy the Kid was shot. My internal homing device was set for Georgia, and I just didn't feel the need or urge to stop. As I was driving along through Arizona and thinking of Lindy ditching me, I wondered if she had planned that the whole time and was just waiting for an excuse to bail out. One thing was for sure, I would have fewer bathroom stops and a lighter load for better gas mileage.

One other thing, though. Now I didn't have anyone to tell my stories to anymore. I would just have to tell them to myself. As I was driving, I began suffering from a little brain damage from all the partying in Las Vegas and the effects of the long road trip. It reminded me of a story about my first years of employment after college.

THEN CAME DAIN BRAMAGE

The title to this story is an adaption from Alex Hawkins' book about his hilarious business ventures after pro football, *Then Came Brain Damage.* Credit for the phrase "dain bramage" goes to a young University of Georgia graduate who once worked for me. She said dain bramage was what happened to college students who imbibed in alcohol too heavily before they graduated.

After graduation from Troy State, I interviewed with several companies and chose Deering Milliken, the textile company located in Spartanburg, South Carolina. Milliken had offered me the unthinkable amount of 9,200 dollars per year to work in their management training program. I remember leaving the interview where I received the official job offer thinking, "How in the hell will I ever be able to spend THAT much money?"

My career with Milliken was short lived, however. Though the management program was excellent, there was something about working a seven day-a-week job, on a swing shift, in Union, South Carolina (population 15,000), that did not appeal to a rambunctious college graduate. When I had to drive forty miles to Spartanburg, South Carolina, to have a good time, I discovered that I was not in the singles mecca of the world.

One day after being chewed out by my boss over an insignificant matter, I went home, went directly to the bathroom mirror, looked at my reflection, and said, "You know, you do have a college education! You don't have to put up with this crap!"

I then sat down and wrote a list of ten things I liked to do and ranked them from one to ten. Not surprisingly, construction and real estate were at the top. Thirty days later, I was back in my hometown of Milledgeville, Georgia, and began framing houses for a company named Allstate Homes with my best friend, Larry Eady. Larry had been a draftsman (house plan drawer) for Allstate. He had a great background in construction, gained from working for his father (Little Cecil Eady) in high school and college. We formed E&S Construction Company, capitalized by the grand total of 1,000 dollars. Now you may think that framing houses doesn't have much to do with a college degree, but framing houses led me directly into a real estate career that is now in its fortieth year.

Allstate Homes, for whom we were framing homes exclusively, was a unique prefabricated house-building company that offered home builders speed and labor savings. At least, that was the sales pitch. Allstate Homes was owned by Walter B. Williams, the long time mayor of Milledgeville. Walter Williams was the consummate "Boss Hog" type of character. All Walter would have needed to qualify for a part in that movie was a white suit and a white straw hat. He was a short individual, but he cut a wide swath across Middle Georgia. Mr. Williams was one of the luckiest guys you ever met. Several times he would go out and buy a piece of property and a few months later, the City of Milledgeville would annex that property into the city, affording access to water and sewage. How lucky can you get?

After a couple of months, Larry and I found out that framing houses was not only hard work, which we had no problem with, but it was also hard to make money. Everything had to be perfect. Allstate paid us a flat fee per house, but we had to pay our workers by the hour. If the truck delivering the home packages was late . . . tough, we had to eat it. Not to mention inconsistent weather patterns and equipment failures like the time we had our whole crew of six guys loaded in one of our trucks driving up Highway 441 toward Athens when the truck's gas tank fell out from under the truck and slid past us into the ditch.

One day as we were framing away, a big Cadillac pulled up on our job site, and Mr. Walter Williams "hisself" stepped out and walked over to the edge of the house where we were setting roof trusses. He stood there for a while, watching us work, then yelled at Larry, "Which one of these knuckleheads is Gary Spillers?" Larry pointed his hammer at me. Mr. Williams then said, "Spillers, what is this I hear about you having a degree in marketing?"

I said, "That's right, I do, but why would you want to know that?"

"Because it's time you start selling these houses instead of framing them. Larry doesn't need you to be his partner; both of y'all will make more money by splitting up. Be in my office next Monday morning, and we will work out a pay plan for you. See you then!"

The next Monday morning, I was in Mr. Williams' office at 8:30 a.m. and was greeted by Mrs. Betty Holsenbeck, Mr. Williams' private secretary. Betty was the mother of a couple of my younger sister's high school friends, so we knew each other casually. She would become one of my life-long friends.

Mr. Williams came blowing into the office around 8:45 a.m. and invited me back into his office. As I walked into his office, I was impressed with the huge size of his private office, which was decorated with quarter horse trophies and family pictures. Walter Williams was a small man, anyway, and this huge desk and office made him look even smaller. But I didn't tell *him* that!

"Spillers, let's get down to business. I know you and Larry have been struggling with this framing business. And quite frankly, it's not your fault. Our deliveries haven't been as crisp and timely as they should be, and our sales haven't been where they should be either. That's what I wanted to talk to you about this morning. Betty, go down the hall and tell Ben (Ben Killingsworth, Allstate's sales manager) to get his ass down here to meet Gary."

Ben was introduced to me and was told that I would be the new salesman to cover the Augusta market that they had talked about.

"Ben, Gary is one of my local boys from here in Milledgeville. He was one hell of a football player for Baldwin High School and went on to be a college football star down at Troy State. As you know, he and Larry Eady have been framing houses for us, so he won't need much training on the product. He majored in marketing, so he understands sales. He should do well for us in a territory where we have no current customers."

No customers! Great, I thought, I either have unlimited opportunities or no chance in hell! On top of that, I didn't think I had ever been to Augusta.

It was agreed that I would spend a couple of days in the plant and learn as much as I could about the sales process and how precise the sales contracts had to be, so that the house would be cut perfectly for the customer. After that, Ben would ride with me a couple of days, calling on builders. Then, I would be out on my own.

When I first pulled into Augusta, Georgia, I had no idea what to think, where to go, or who to talk to. Sales brochures highlighting my company? You've got to be kidding.

Ben and I went to the first phone booth we could find and took the phone book. That phone book became my prospect list. We then began randomly looking up the office addresses on a map we bought at the Shell service station on Washington Road. Needless to say, we weren't very successful that first day because all the builders were out on the job sites and most of them didn't have offices anyway. This was a couple of years before car phones were available at an affordable price; in 1971, only the very rich had car phones.

So the next day, we began calling on Realtors and anyone who might be able to introduce us to builders. The first company that we called on was Channel Realty. Cliff Channel had a cast of characters working for him that was unrivaled in the Augusta area. They were not only tops in real estate sales, but also in partying! Cliff, a former college baseball star at the University of Georgia, was a very energetic guy and was a hard worker, and he was joined by the cast of characters that worked for Channel Realty such as Bill Heirs, Jack Hodges, Sonny Casey, Tim Hill, and Dick Wimmer.

The day we called on Cliff, he wasn't in, and we were sent to talk to his commercial agent, Bert Storey. Since that time, Bert has become one of the most successful shopping center developers, owners, and managers in the Southeast. I still count him as one of my good friends today. The whole time I worked in Augusta, I stayed in touch with Bert and we still call each other every month or so. Though Bert was not a builder, he referred me to many guys who were, such as Arthur Holmes.

Arthur Holmes was one of the most interesting individuals I have ever or will ever meet in my life. Arthur was divorced and was "a man around town" with the ladies. He took pride in keeping up with everybody's business and held court daily out on the sidewalk in front of his downtown office, located at the corner of Broad Street and Eighth Street, with all of his buddies. They checked out the ample number of attractive ladies scurrying to get lunch and get back to their offices.

A legend around Augusta, Georgia, Arthur Holmes began earning his reputation early in his career while working for the ultimate real estate agent incubator, Trotter Realty. Arthur worked as a floundering new agent at Trotter alongside Cliff Channel who told this tale to Bert Storey about

Arthur's, shall we say, unorthodox sales approach with customers.

It seems that Arthur was missing a much-needed item when he got into the real estate business that most all other real estate agents had . . . a car. This didn't bother Arthur one bit. He just concentrated his listing and sales efforts to specific areas along the Augusta bus line, which went by Trotter Realty and his home. For property searches outside of the bus line area, the customer was required to furnish the transportation if he was to work with Sir Arthur!

According to legend, one day Arthur took a sales call that Cliff overheard. The calling customer inquired about the availability of an inexpensive three-bedroom home with a fenced back yard, just off the bus line. Arthur wrapped up the phone call with a promise to the potential buyer that he would work hard to find just the right property for him and hung up the phone. Cliff, not wanting to be too nosy, asked Arthur, "Don't you have a house listed over on Oak Street that is exactly what that customer wanted to purchase?"

Arthur acknowledged that he did, then turned to Cliff and said, "Cliff, if I had blurted out to that guy that I have exactly what he wanted, he wouldn't have believed me. This way, when I call him back in a couple of days, he will think I worked my ass off to find his dream home and will buy it on the spot, especially after I show him a couple of other overpriced 'dogs'."

Arthur was short in stature, wore horned-rim glasses, and always carried a pistol with him, which sometimes got him in trouble. Arthur had a heart condition and walked every day. During one of his afternoon walks, a neighborhood dog attacked him and was attempting to take a chunk out of Arthur's leg. Arthur brandished his pistol and shot the dog in the foot, then continued walking home, as did the wounded dog minus a couple of toes. Arthur shortly got a visit from the local police who agreed with him that they would have probably done the same thing, but they had to cite him for firing a gun within the city limits.

On another occasion, Arthur, who was by this time buying my package houses, had gotten an urgent call from his homebuilding foreman, "Big Earl" who always wore overalls and a straw hat on the job. "Big Earl" considered himself to be an old-time quality builder, and he didn't like Arthur buying package houses from me (probably because it threatened his livelihood somewhat). As soon as we got on the site, we found Big Earl cussing Allstate's foreman, telling him he was continuing to "fuck up the house."

Arthur calmly walked up to Big Earl and snatched the plans out of his hand and asked Big Earl to show him the problem. Once the plans were turned right side up and Big Earl got on the right page . . . voila . . . there was no problem. Arthur was pissed! It was lunchtime, and he was missing valuable chick-grading time downtown at the corner.

Arthur pulled out his gun . . . "Oh shit," I thought, "he is going to shoot Big Earl!"

He pointed the gun to the sky and fired two shots, as all work stopped on the job site. Arthur then boomed to Big Earl, "Now that I have your attention, you stupid son of a bitch, I want you to know that you have about as much business walking around this job site with a set of house plans in your hand, as I have walking around Memorial Hospital with a fucking stethoscope around my neck!"

With customers like Arthur, my business developed nicely in Augusta. When I first went there, no builders were buying package homes, but I expanded Allstate Home's market, and we were shipping to Augusta on a regular basis. I developed, through good people like Arthur Holmes, a niche market for very expensive homes to be panelized in our plant and then shipped to job sites at places like the exquisite West Lake Country Club. The founding member of West Lake was Mr. Cheatum Hodges who became a very good customer of mine and Allstate Homes.

Augusta, Georgia, could not have been a better training ground for me as a salesperson. For the first order I took, the builder said, "I don't want one house, I want five houses."

Ben Killingsworth, my sales manager, was with me that day. I got the nervous shakes so bad that I couldn't write the order. Ben had to write it for me. Nothing like that had ever happened to me before and hasn't happened to me since. I guess I choked under pressure of having to write five contracts.

****

Wednesday at The Masters in Augusta was a magical day in the early '70s. Back then, anyone could get in the hallowed grounds for very little to see golf's top heroes in action for the par three tournaments. Draft beer was only fifty cents, and much beer was consumed on that Wednesday. It was also a virtual hit parade for some of the nicest looking and most available ladies–not only from Augusta, but the whole Southeast.

During the next year, in 1972, things began to change at Allstate Homes. New management was taking over, and Mr. Williams seemed to lose interest in being involved on a daily basis, perhaps from losing voting control of the company or just getting tired of the day-to-day grind a manufacturing business brings with it.

During the summer of 1972, Mr. Williams called me into his office and told me that he was selling Allstate Homes to an investment group and that he was going to start a new real estate company in Milledgeville. He wanted Mike Jackson, another Milledgeville boy who worked for Allstate, and me to be his first two real estate agents.

This sounded great to me because every real estate broker or agent that I knew in Augusta drove a brand new Cadillac or a Mercedes Benz. They had to be making good money!

In 1972, you did not have to attend a state-approved real estate course before you took the exam. You just showed up to take the test; if you passed, you were in!

Arthur Holmes gave me an extra office in his offices to study anytime I wanted to use it. I was still working my Allstate job when I took the test. Mike Jackson and I took the real estate license test on the same day. He passed and I flunked the test by two points. I then rededicated myself to study harder and passed the test the following month of September.

Mr. Williams went through with the sale of Allstate, and we began Southern Classic Properties in the fall of 1972. I didn't come onboard until December, selling my first house on January 1, 1973. I called Betty Holsenbeck, our secretary, at home on New Year's morning at 8:30 a.m. and asked her to come over to the office to type the contract for my customers to sign. Betty bitched all the way over there, but she was awful proud that I had sold that house for the new company.

Over the next six months, I sold almost a million dollars worth of real estate for Southern Classic Properties and was doing well.

Working for Walter Williams (and I might as well add, Betty Holsenbeck, because she was Walter's right-hand person and was a heavy influence on Mr. Williams' decisions) at Southern Classic Properties was a blast. After Mike Jackson and I got our real estate licenses in 1972, there was only one other real estate broker practicing in Milledgeville at that time, and that was Alton Rogers who worked for Allfarm Sales out of Gray, Georgia. All of Alton's business was centered in the Milledgeville market.

Though Southern Classic was a fun place to work, I did not necessarily learn a lot of good work habits from Mr. Williams. Every afternoon at 5:00 p.m. was happy hour at Southern Classic. On cue at 5 p.m., Walter would bark out to Betty, "Get me a Schlitz malt liquor." That was the signal that all work for the day was suspended, and it was time to relax in Mr. Williams' gigantic office, have a beverage and talk about the day's activities and politics. (Mr. Williams political supporters were regulars at all time of the day and for happy hour.) Gus Pursley, Wendell Hardie, Wayne Ogletree, and Charles Cheeves, among a cast of others, could always be depended upon for a good story or some political inside news so critical to Walter.

Sometimes the meetings weren't started all that pleasantly. One day at 5;00 p.m., Walter came busting through the front door and hollered to Betty, "Get me one of them goddamned Schlitz Maltz liquors!" He then blurted out so that everyone in the office could hear him, "I don't know who that goddamned Bob Daugherty thinks he is, but by God, he is going to learn that in Milledgeville, Georgia you can't fuck the FUCKER!"

Apparently, Bob had beaten Walter in securing a very profitable land deal and gotten it zoned right out from under Walter's nose. Walter didn't appreciate competition, especially in his own backyard. Walter Williams was all about Milledgeville and cared and knew little about markets outside of Baldwin County. He attempted to rule over his fiefdom with an iron hand. Developers like Bob Daugherty were unwelcome competition, mainly because they were probably smarter real estate men and worked harder than Walter. After Walter and Bob had words over this land deal where Bob prevailed, he was heard to tell Walter, "Walter, the sun don't shine on the same dog's ass every day!"

Another day, Walter was disgruntled at Wayne Harris and Ronnie Waddell (a couple of local real estate hustlers) for getting a key piece of lake property under contract for development. Walter opined to us during one our many happy hour meetings, "Those damn fools. They have overpaid for that land. Don't they know it's *long distance* up there in Putnam County?" Ironically, Wayne and Ronnie "flipped" the deal to Bob Daugherty, and they all made a killing, much to Walter's chagrin.

One night after our "warm up" happy hour ended at Southern Classic, I met a couple of buddies at the Holiday Inn lounge for drinks. Seated a couple of tables over was Bob Green, one of the owners of the Inn, and some of his cronies. Bob Green, a local lawyer and one of Walter's political enemies, was openly backing a new man for mayor of Milledgeville named Bob Rice. Bob Green was a contentious sort (imagine that, being a lawyer and all), and as soon as I sat down, he started throwing political barbs my way, which I ignored. Then, in a booming voice worthy of courtroom praise, he said, "Bob Rice will be the next mayor of Milledgeville!" The challenge was directed straight at me. I ignored him again, which pissed Green off! Then in an even louder voice, he said again, "Bob Rice will be the next mayor of Milledgeville!"

After that one, I had heard enough. I stood up, looked directly at Green, and said, "Bob Rice will never be mayor of Milledgeville as long as Walter Williams wants to be Mayor!"

Green then says, "Well, Big Man, do you want to bet on it? I'll bet you 500 dollars."

I said, "Hell yes, I'll bet you," whereupon Green stood up and started counting cash out on the bar table.

I said, "Whoa, Buddy. I don't have that kind of cash on me."

Green then said, "I didn't figure you had the cash to back up your chickenshit bet!"

I looked at Green, wondering if I should go ahead and put him out of his obvious misery right in the middle of his own bar or let him live another day. I chose the latter. I then walked over to his table as the tension began to mount in the bar and looked him in the eye and said simply, "I will be back!"

As I was leaving, I heard Green laughing and telling his group of political experts, "We'll not be seeing him anymore tonight."

As they all had a good laugh at my expense, I left the bar.

It was about 10:00 p.m. and well past Mr. Williams' bedtime, but I drove straight to his house, went to the back door, and rang the doorbell. As expected, Mrs. Eugenia Williams came to the door in her bathrobe and, upon recognizing me, opened the door and invited me in. I apologized to her for coming over so late but told her there was there was an important matter that I had to talk to Mr. Williams about.

About this time, Mr. Williams appeared in his robe. "Spillers, this better be important!"

I told him what happened and he didn't say a word. He just turned to Mrs. Williams and said, "Eugenia, go get 1,000 dollars in cash out of the safe." He turned back to me and said, "Double the bet on the bastard and let me know what happens as soon as it is over."

Ms. Eugenia showed back up and counted ten crisp 100-dollar bills out in my hand. I thanked them both and headed back to the Holliday Inn lounge, where I was certain Bob and his entourage were well oiled by now and still reveling in their earlier victory.

I was right. When I walked back into the lounge, Bob was holding court and they were all laughing and having a good ole time. That was, until they saw me walk back into the bar.

When I walked back into the lounge and straight over to Bob's table, everything quickly got deathly quiet. You could have heard a pin drop in that bar. I began counting the crisp, 100-dollar bills out on Bob's table.

Then, I said, "Green, I have considered your offer to bet with all that cash you have in your pocket, and I want to double your bet that Bob Rice will not be the next mayor of Milledgeville."

Green didn't know what to do. His face turned red, and he began to sweat. His bet had not only been called, it had been doubled—right in his face and in front of his friends. I then said, "Put up or shut up, *Big Man*!"

Bob Green then did one of the most surprising things I have ever seen a man under pressure resort to. He stood up and yelled at the bartenders, "Joe and Wilbert, go call the sheriff. This man is in here trying to gamble illegally in my bar!"

I reached over and picked up the cash and said, "I knew you were too chickenshit to bet when it counted. And, by the way, Bob Rice won't be the next mayor!" (And he wasn't!)

As I left the bar for the second time that night, there was no laughing and guffawing coming from Green's table. With all the egg Green had on his face, he could have served breakfast to his cronies!

I didn't call Mr. Williams back. I drove straight over to his house and gave him the money back, then told him what happened. He slapped me on the shoulder and said, "Spillers, I appreciate what you did, but it sounds like we may have a real mayor's race this time. We had better start getting ready. See you on Monday, Big Man!"

On Monday morning, the Holiday Inn caper was the talk of the town, and no one enjoyed it any more than Betty Holsenbeck. Betty, a very attractive lady in her early forties, was like a second mother to all of us and was our "main most" cheerleader.

Betty was also a woman ahead of her time. At the early age of eighteen, she was not only flying airplanes, she was doing it solo with very little radio or any radar direction. On a simple little flight around Baldwin and Wilkinson Counties one day, she got lost and ended up being forced to land at what is now Hartsfield-Jackson International Airport south of Atlanta. It didn't upset Betty at all. She just refueled, got her bearings, and took off again toward middle Georgia. No problem.

There were rumors of a romantic tie with Walter Williams and Betty over the years, but I think it was mostly speculation or jealousy that Walter had the sharpest secretary in town working for him.

****

One morning, I was in the real estate office when the phone rang and this mature-sounding country woman said, "I would like ta speak to somebody that can sell me a parcel of land. Bout a hundred acres should do it. Me and Pa done live down here in Wilkinson County wid tha young'uns and we need us some mo room."

She introduced herself as Miss Salley Reid, and she wanted to know when we could go look at some land.

I told her that I had 110 acres of land fairly close to where she lived and that I could show it to her tomorrow. She said that would be fine. Could I pick her and pa up to go look at it? I told her I could and got directions to her house. I went back and checked with Betty Holsenbeck who was from Wilkinson County. Betty made a few calls, and the word was that the old lady had money and could probably buy some land if she "took a notion."

The next morning, I pulled up at the appointed address to pick up Ma, Pa, and whoever else would choose to ride. I felt as if I'd gone back in time fifty years. These people lived in an old shotgun, country house with no paint on the walls; the pillars up under the house were old, stacked fieldstone. Chickens, dogs, cats, and nekkid young'uns were running every which way! I swear it was a scene from the old Snuffy Smith cartoons, only worse.

Miss Salley came out and introduced herself. She was dressed just as I had imagined in a long country dress with an apron attached to it, and she was wearing a sunbonnet.

Then Pa appeared. Pa was an elderly man with worn overalls and a big straw hat. Pa was so old-looking that it would be a good bet that he didn't purchase any green bananas at the grocery store for fear that he might die before they became ripe.

Miss Salley says, "Mr. Spillers, if you don't mind, just me, Pa, and our eldest girl is gonna ride with you this morning."

"That's fine," I said.

Before we left, Ma had to bark out instructions to the other elder children to look out for the young'uns and to keep 'em up under the porch and out of the sun.

Finally, we were off to look at the land I had close by, which was 110 acres of the ugliest Wilkinson County land I had ever seen, but it had a good price on it. I drove straight to the property, pulled off the road, and stopped.

"Here it is."

Ma stepped out of the car, then motioned for Pa and the eldest girl and they all just stood there and looked at the property in amazement.

She turned around and said, "It is beautiful! I want it. Me and Pa will go over to Macon to talk to Mr. Jim Walter about buildin' us a house on it. Then we can trade with you on the land."

So, with that tenuous agreement in place, I took them home to the bizarre house that they lived in and hustled on back to the office.

I didn't hear anything from Ma for a couple of days. Then, one morning the phone rang and it was Ma. "I'm sorry I hadn't called you," she said, "but Pa done up and died on me!"

"Oh my God, I am so sorry," I said.

Ma thanked me and said that once things got settled down, if that land was still there, she still wanted to get it. I said okay and wished her my best.

A couple of weeks later, the phone rang as I was walking out the door with some clients for a day-long showing. Betty said it was Ma from down in Wilkinson County. I took a minute to speak to her. Ma said she was ready to do something on that land, but she wanted to go look at it one more time. I told her I was tied up that day, but I would try to get another agent to show the property to her.

Mike Jackson, who was a loud, show-boat type of salesman with a big new fancy car, volunteered to take them—based on Betty's prior research that they had the money to buy the land. I told Mike about the house and the strange offspring, so he'd be prepared when he pulled up there.

When I got back to the office that afternoon, Mike's car was in the parking lot and seemed to be even cleaner than usual. As I entered the office, Mike was all over me, cursing and raising hell with me about sticking him with those country bumpkins.

After I got Mike settled down, he told me what happened. "It was just like you said. I got to the house and young'uns of all ages running among the chickens and the cats and dogs. Well, Miss Salley decided that we would take the eldest girl again if I didn't mind if she took a dip (of snuff) and I said I didn't, and she wanted the eldest boy along, which I said seemed fine."

"So what are you pissed off about, Mike?" I asked.

"You are about to find out, my friend," he said. "After we looked at the land and we walked a good bit more than y'all did, we got back in the car. As we continued down the road, I noticed that the eldest girl was trying to say something from the back seat, but she had her lips packed with snuff. She began going uuuummm . . . uuummmm . . . Then, all of a sudden, she went into a higher tone and going MMMMMMmming . . . MMMMMing . . . I didn't know what was happening in that back seat, and I didn't want to know. Then the smell hit me, and then the coughing began. Apparently, the eldest boy got carsick and was throwing up on the eldest girl, who was trying to alert us with the mmmmings. Then, the eldest girl got sick and starting coughing and spitting snuff juice all over the back seat of my brand new car!

Mike said he just pulled over by the side of the road got out and walked about a quarter of a mile up the road to get away from the mess that was once his back seat. When he got back to the car, Ma "had done tore" the front parts off her and the eldest girls' dresses, using their dress fronts to clean up the mess. Mike took them home, dumped them as fast as possible, and sought out the closest detail shop available.

Mike didn't want to hear predictions of when or if Ma was going to buy that land. He just didn't want any more of it.

I did talk to Ma a few other times, but she never was successful getting Mr. Jim Walter to build on that land for her. As for Jackson, he was thereafter skeptical of any more land referrals from me!

****

About as fast as my career got started with Southern Classic Properties, it ended within eight months. One of my friends from high school, Bill Harrington, who had attended the University of Georgia, had moved to Atlanta and was making "big money" selling a relatively new product for the Atlanta market called condominiums. Bill was working for a development company named Crow Pope & Land. Bill had encouraged me on several occasions to consider coming to Atlanta and joining him.

On more than one occasion, I had visited Bill in Atlanta and (much to his wife Elaine's chagrin), we would go out on the town in and around Atlanta. The scenery was always stunning to me. I'm talking about the good-looking women scenery—not the landscape. At that time, I was set up pretty good in Milledgeville, but the lure of big city with its big-money opportunities, bright lights, and good-looking women was just to big of an adventure to turn down. Plus, I had already gone through most of the available, single, and attractive women in Milledgeville and what few were left that appealed to me were smart enough not to have anything to do with me!

It should be easy to see where this is going. I resigned at Southern Classic, which was not a popular decision with Mr. Williams, but he had other salespeople coming onboard like Tom Hines, Henry Sheppard, and Bill Craig. So I moved to Atlanta, taking a job with Crow Pope & Land, selling condominiums in a small condo development in Marietta called The Fairways.

The first night in Atlanta was a single man's dream. As I was unpacking my furniture, the neighbors came over to introduce themselves. They were two, drop-dead good-looking flight attendants for Delta Airlines. Both loved to play tennis, which I was really into at the time. We ended up playing tennis later that day; then we grilled some steaks and shared a couple of bottles of wine. As a coup de grace, the better looking one of the two came over to my place and stayed the night with me.

The next day, my first day on the job, I sold a condo to the first person who walked through the door. Had I died and gone to heaven or what? Pinch me. Man, this can't be happening. Can it? Well it was, and it did.

Later that month, mortgage money ran out in the state of Georgia, which was the beginning of a roller coaster ride for the real estate business in Atlanta, Georgia, for the next three to four years. There was a popular saying during this period: "You can always tell a real estate man in Atlanta when he drives up in his Mercedes Benz with bald tires and a hole in the trunk where the telephone used to be."

But my favorite recollection of those days involves the LSD deals. During the '73-'76 period, most all Realtors carried LSD deals around in our briefcases. LSD deals were defined as "real estate deals that were so bad it would take someone under the influence of LSD to even consider buying them!"

The next three years was an interesting time to live in Atlanta, Georgia, especially for a single person. The real estate market was upside down most of those three years of the mid '70s. During this period, from 1973 to 1976, I struggled to survive, going from deal to deal and searching for something to do that was both interesting and profitable.

I worked in residential real estate, land syndication, timeshares, insurance, resort home sales, officiating youth football, or anything to make a dollar to live and party another day, while attempting to avoid "Dain Bramage" in good ole "Hotlanta."

One group of guys that I worked with during that period was a lot of fun, and most all of us have remained good friends. These guys were in the land and syndication business. The main two partners were Ron Slack and Ray Cosby. Oddly, Ron was a University of Florida graduate and football star, and Ray was a Florida State guy, which caused much bickering and kidding throughout the year. Almost every guy who worked there was an ex-jock of some college sport. Pete Baily and Norm Cates played football for Lou Holtz at North Carolina State. Bill Harrington played at Georgia. Bobby Hatfield played baseball at Florida State. "Fig" Newton played basketball at Florida State. Other regulars around that office included Evan Jennings and the crafty real estate pro Ray McPhail.

"Fig" Newton was a legend around the Atlanta bar scene, along with his buddy Jim Morton. These guys were huge, both about 6 feet, 4 inches tall and 250 pounds. In a crowded bar one night, some guy who had no regard for his own life pissed Fig off about something and then, instead of being killed, would be surprised when Fig chose to piss on his leg. The guy never knew what was going on until the piss soaked though his pants leg.

One time, an ex-girlfriend got Fig kicked out of an apartment that he really liked. The girl was a flight attendant and traveled a lot. So Fig waited until she left on a lengthy trip, searched for and found a maggot-infested, dead dog, and deposited it on the console of her car. When the girl got home a few days later, you could imagine her face when she discovered her newest passenger. Fig said he thought the lady ended up having to get some psychiatric evaluations after finding the well-seasoned canine in her car.

Another time, Fig was in Las Vegas one night when he chose to invest in a familiar-looking hooker. "Don't we know each other?" Fig questioned.

"Not on your life, Buster," the hooker retorted as they made their way to Fig's room.

After their tryst and in the elevator on the way down to the lobby, Fig again says, "I don't care what you say, I feel like we have known each other in the past."

The lady of the night then said, "Fig, if you must know, that piece of ass you just paid me 100 dollars for up in that room, I gave to you free in Atlanta three months ago!"

I told you he was a legend.

****

Enough of the reminiscing. It was time to get back to Georgia and get my life started again.

Rick Hartnett, the very scallawag that sold me the Green Pig, and I were slated to move in with Ray Cosby who owned a mini-mansion down on Defoors Ferry Road in Atlanta. Ray was the consummate bachelor, who was extremely nervous about dating girls over twenty years of age. I never could figure out whether it was because the young bodies turned him on or whether he just couldn't carry on an intelligent conversation with any woman over twenty. I think it was both.

The house was really cool, though, and Ray would top that off with building a swimming pool out back in the shape of a woman. This pool was amazing and a little weird and featured breasts that each shot out vertical streams of water. The head of the pool was a Jacuzzi and on the other end . . . well, I will just let your imagination take over from here.

Fun times and serious work opportunities lay ahead. I guess I was getting a little homesick for ole Atlanta.

CHAPTER NINE

I was "gaining ground" as Wilbur Bell used to say. I had already made it through the badlands of Arizona and was pushing east, past Albuquerque through the New Mexico Desert. Off to my right was a tumbleweed, which was keeping up with the Green Pig at about sixty-five miles per hour, pushed by a strong eastward desert wind.

I thought, how much like me . . . it was amazing what my current life had in common with that tumbleweed. About that time, the tumbleweed hit a fence post and stopped. I slammed on the brakes, stopped the car, and retrieved the tumbleweed, then placed it in the back of my car with all the other junk I had collected on my extended trip.

About sixty miles down the interstate close to Tucumcari, New Mexico, a dreadful thing happened. A New Mexico State trooper pulled me over. I got out of the car and was in the process of taking out my license when the trooper told me to back off and stay by my car.

Riding with him were an Indian and a German Shepherd dog. The Indian was dressed in worn jeans, old leather boots, and a leather vest covered with beads. He wore a black cowboy hat with an eagle feather stuck in the band. He didn't seem amused as he crawled up onto the hood of the trooper car, where he crossed his legs and arms and just sat there staring straight ahead without saying a word. The dog also sat at attention by the trooper car.

After finally checking my credentials, the trooper asked if it was allright for him to search my vehicle.

"No sir, help yourself," I said, but my heart began racing. At that moment, I remembered that in the trunk of my car was a bag of old pot. It was *really bad* because Whit had given it to me back in Aspen because he couldn't give it away, much less sell it. My guess is that it was *so bad*, the dog couldn't smell it. As the trooper was searching the car, he actually picked up the sack that the pot was in and moved it to the side. My heart was in my throat. I could picture myself in a New Mexico chain gang as a pot smuggler.

After the brief search, the trooper turned to me and said, "It looks like you are clean. But Son, answer one question for me. What in the hell are you doing with a tumbleweed in the back of your car?"

As the trooper and his two faithful riders pulled away, I wondered aloud, "How far is it to the next exit with a bathroom so that I could have the opportunity to clean the shit out of my pants?"

As I continued on eastward down I-40, my mind became flooded with all the characters I had met on this trip and the many characters that have been involved in my stories.

One really outstanding fellow that I haven't told a tale about is C.P. Edwards of Bremen, Georgia. C.P. was best friends with Wilbur Bell, the uncle of my runnin' mate Barry Bucklew. Both C.P. and Wilbur loved to go to Panama City to go deep-sea fishing for "kings and snappers." They also enjoyed drinking and carousing in the bars of Panama City. But make no mistake about it, they were dead serious fishermen, and they were out of bed at 4:30 a.m., ready to head to the boats to get as early a start as possible—no matter how much they drank or what time they got in.

On my first fishing trip with these guys, I didn't know anyone but Wilbur. Barry had told me about C.P., however, and what a bad-ass legend he was around Bremen. I wasn't impressed with all that small-town bragging because I was pretty much a bad ass myself!

On this trip, Barry and I drove our own car and got into the hotel while all the other guys were already out to dinner. So we immediately hit the bars and stayed out until around 2:00 to 3:00 a.m. with a couple of beach bunnies.

At 4:30 the next morning, the alarm clock went off, sounding to me like an atomic bomb. I immediately shut it off and threw it into the corner of the room.

Barry said, "We might as well get up 'cause Wilbur will be by shortly. He's probably been up for an hour already."

Sure enough, a few minutes later, Wilbur was banging on the door, and Barry made the mistake of letting him in. As soon as Wilbur got in the room, he was acting like an old barnyard rooster. "Come on, you pussies, it's time to go fishing, let's go guys . . . com'on, let's go!"

I then made a near-fatal mistake. From the warm comfort of my hotel bed, I muttered, "I don't think I am going fishing this morning."

Wilbur said, "Looks like we need to go get C.P."

I said, "Bullshit, I'm going back to sleep, and I ain't goin' fishing."

Famous last words.

I had not met C.P . . . but I was about to! A few rays of sunlight were just making their way through our hotel room door, from which Wilbur was now directing traffic. All of a sudden, all the light left the door because the biggest human I had ever seen came through the door, blocking out all the light as he entered the room.

The creature said, "Wilbur, which one of these pussies says he is not going fishing this morning?"

Wilbur pointed to me. By this time, Barry already knew the drill and was struggling to get his best fishing clothes on. C.P. walked over to my bed, grabbed me by my ankle and popped my whole 210-pound body like a maid would pop a bedsheet.

I got the message. I was going fishing!

C.P. and I became good friends after that little episode and are still friends today. One of C.P.'s best lines is, "You know I was a great lover, and you know I must have been, because after I make love to 'em, they never call again (not even to complain)."

All artists have their signature pieces of work, and C.P. was no different. Once, when the boys at Am Vets Post 55 (The Double Nickel in Bremen) were having a few beers, the subject of cremation came up. C.P. waded in with his opinion on the subject. "Well boys, I'm not so sure about this cremation thing and having my ashes spread across a lake, river, or old homeplace. My take on the matter is that I would hope that they cremate me allright, but then I would want them to grind my ashes up with douche powder so I could be run through that thang one more time before I go!"

It's like a phrase from one of Jimmy Buffett's songs: 'People's lives change like the weather, but a legend never dies!'

****

Traveling through the Texas panhandle, I began looking for some good country music when . . . what did I hear on the radio? . . . A couple just outside Amarillo, Texas, have two end zone tickets for the Dallas Cowboys' playoff game with the Los Angeles Rams in Dallas for the next day, the nineteenth of December. They will sell these tickets at face value of twelve dollars each.

As soon as I heard this, I felt sorry for the West Texas couple who wouldn't be able to attend the religious services put on by the Dallas Cowboys and the Los Angeles Rams. But this could be a windfall. Those tickets would be worth two or three times face value of twelve dollars each, just before the game. I was headed through Amarillo, and I could easily stop and buy the tickets and make it to Dallas by game time the next day.

My plan was to stop and buy the tickets, take State Route 287 from Amarillo down through Wichita Falls to Dallas, show up at Texas Stadium the next day, and sell the tickets. I would make a killing, then hit the road again.

The first part of my plan worked perfectly. I secured the tickets, then showed up at Texas Stadium the next day where a parking spot a mile from the stadium cost me five dollars. As I was walking toward the stadium, I ran into someone I knew from college, Lee Fong. Lee was one of our football cheerleaders at Troy State University and a great guy. He was now living in Dallas and working in sales. He was also into hustling football tickets on the side.

I said, "Lee, you are in luck. I have two good tickets in the end zone that I will sell you for twenty-five dollars each."

Lee laughed. "No thanks, Gary. I don't know if you have heard or not, but they are now televising this game on local TV, and the local ticket prices have plummeted. You will be lucky if you can *give* those tickets away."

"Oh shit!" I thought, "What am I going to do now?"

Lee was right. I held those tickets up in the air so long I got arm cramps. After it was evident that the tickets were not going to sell, my only option was to go to the game myself, which I did with an empty seat next to me. I had a good (albeit expensive) experience, and I think the Rams won the game anyway. Who cares?

The next day, I was on the road early, headed east on I-20 through Texas, Louisiana, Mississippi, and Alabama. I was stopping over in Birmingham to spend the night with Tommy Arrington to watch the Liberty Bowl game, featuring Bear Bryant's Crimson Tide against the UCLA Bruins. This would be one of Bear's last bowl games. He would soon retire as the college football coach with the most wins of all time.

The drive from Dallas was a long one, but was shortened somewhat by a phone conversation I had with a good friend Donnie Hampton in Atlanta. Donnie had just taken over the management of a residential mortgage company and had a job waiting on me as soon as I got back to Atlanta.

Even with that good news, the memories of the trip and the stories that had been told and the good times that had been had were flooding my brain. The most distinct memories were of the people who willingly or unwillingly participated in this trip and these tales.

"OUR LIVES CHANGE LIKE THE WEATHER . . .

BUT A LEGEND NEVER DIES!"

—*JIMMY BUFFETT*

WHO'S WHO

- The polo horse and rider from T.G.I. Friday's - last seen headed up Roswell Road.

- Rufus Guthrie - died of brain cancer in the mid '90s. A football legend playing for Coach Bobby Dodd and the Georgia Tech Yellow Jackets in the '60s.

- Barry Buckelew - somewhat retired up on Lake Lanier. Has a daughter, Brett, a graduate of the University of Georgia and a son, Bart, who is currently enrolled at Georgia. We still get together to "cut the fool" and talk about Wilbur Bell and C.P. Edwards.

- Wilbur Bell - my very good friend - died in 1988 of cancer. An absolute delight to be around, he was a point man carrying a Thompson Submachine Gun in World War II and, according to Wilber, "knocked many a gook loose" with it in the Philippines.

- Tommy Arrington - lives down in Mobile. Still working for and about to retire from the same company that he wouldn't leave to go out West with me thirty-five years ago. He and his wife, Jane, have two daughters and a son.

- Lionel Ed Rainey - he and Miss Virginia live in "GRAINVILLE," Alabama. They have two grown sons. Still plays golf as a second income stream. Last time we talked, he hadn't been back to the Dykes Lounge or the Carriage Inn. At least he won't admit it if he has!

- Peter Hendricks - last seen at my wedding in 1981. He and Judy moved to England, and I have never heard from them since.

- "Dodo" Hollis - now owns THE Milledgeville Pool Room that still sells legendary chili dogs.

- Howell Horton - still cutting hair and looking down the street every day to see if the Auburn Tiger is coming back! He's not my mom's neighbor anymore, but they stay in touch.

- Jack Maddox - currently successfully working his way through some health issues and goes coon hunting every chance he gets. Jack says Bill Massee still has that big fish's asshole on his truck as a fan belt.

- Bill Massee - duly elected and very popular long-term Sheriff of Baldwin County.

- Wex Wabbit (Lex Sellers) - evolved from being a college derelict to selling Yellow Pages and becoming one of the top salespeople in the country. Married Elaine Griffin, a Milledgeville girl, and they had a son named Griffin, who is now a golf pro. Lex was tragically killed in a car wreck out at Twin Bridges on Lake Sinclair in the late '70s. Elaine eventually remarried one of Lex's good friends, Steve Comer, and they reside on the lake in Milledgeville.

- Jack Smith - played pro football a couple of years with the Philadelphia Eagles. Bought Lefty's Bar in Troy, then eventually settled down in Perry, Georgia, to become a successful builder and developer. Married a Troy girl, Sarah Nave, and they have a son and daughter.

- Johnny Cowart - former teammate who worships me because he never had to make tackles when he played defensive back behind me. He is in just one of the stories, but it would have hurt his feelings if he wasn't in the book.

- Jim "Moe" Gillespie - became "cabbage-head master cabbage grower" up in Clayton, Georgia. Married to Iris Gilmore, also a Troy State graduate, and they have three beautiful daughters.

- "Cool Head" Jimmy Hedrick - became a nurse down in Savannah. Has a beautiful daughter named Leah who is his best friend. Jimmy heads up the Risk

Management Department of St. Joseph's Candler Hospital in Savannah. He is still a cool dude! Is yet to be invited back to drive a Lyncoach truck to ANY destination!

- "Slimey" Spikes - got a job out of college with Tom's Peanuts and transferred to Virginia Beach, Virginia. He is supposed to be doing well.

- Sonny Hendricks - also went from being a college derelict and bowling machine hustler to become very successful in the mechanical contracting business in Florida. Made up the famous line, "Hey, Spools, me and you just like this," holding up two fingers squeezed together. "You got a dollar - I got a dollar." Sonny was always short on his dollar in college.

- Steve Stephens - referred to as Stevie Weavie, Steve Steverson, and many other nicknames I am sure. I don't know what happened to Steve. At one time, he had a successful investment banking business in California, then moved back to Georgia. He and Nicki divorced.

- Nicki Spase Stephens - still good-looking and lives in Athens, Georgia, and teaches school. Her two sons, Silas and Bradley, are in Puerto Rico and California.

- Larry Eady - stayed in Milledgeville, married Georgia College girl Cheryl Brewer, and they have three beautiful daughters. Became a successful builder/-

developer and grandfather. Still gets nosebleeds when he crosses the Baldwin County line on trips.

- Wayne Weaver - settled in Milledgeville and became a builder and "coffee club" host where he and his constituents attempt to top Soda Pop Wilson's courthouse tale on a daily basis . . . at last reading, nobody has come close!

- Billy Cordoza - lived in LA a few more years after my visit and then "went East, young man" to New York City. Billy is in the clothing business and has been living in Connecticut for 25 years.

- Charly Steele - hasn't been and doesn't plan on ever coming back to Milledgeville. He got away with his life the last time he was here . . . but just barely!

- Larry Spillers - big brother extraordinaire . . . has always been there when I needed him and vice versa . . . a man of tremendous respect around Milledgeville, Georgia, he just has a weak stomach for moonshine! But so did his buddy Barney Beall.

- Fig (Harland) Newton - living and working in the Tampa Bay area.

- Jenna Stubbs - Living happily in Manhattan Beach, California. Has three grown kids and is currently getting back to her passion for professional dancing!

- Bryna McNeely - Also living on the beach in California, married and doing well.

- Lindy Stevens - have no clue!

- Sim Byrd - probably the single most important athlete to ever suit up at Troy University. Sim and his teammates, along with Coach Billy Atkins, turned the tide of Troy from being a pitiful loser into one of the most feared competitors in college football on every level! The 1968 National Championship team proved to the world that Troy could compete. The teams, coaches, and administration staff that followed have also done their part in molding Troy University into the winner it is today! But Sim and the boys in the fall of 1968 got it all started in the right direction!

- Coach Billy Atkins - left Troy in 1972 to go back into pro coaching with the Buffalo Bills. Died unexpectedly in a hotel room while exercising in 1994. A brilliant coach and a good person, Coach Atkins was responsible for laying the groundwork for turning Troy University into the football power it is today!

- Max Howell - offensive line coach and head recruiter for the Red Wave. Later went into Sports Radio broadcasting and has carved out a loyal following around the Southeast. Lately, a tailgating cookbook author.

- Phillip Creel - defensive coach for the Red Wave. If I heard "THAT'S THE BEST JOB YOU EVER DID" and "HIT EM IN THE MOUTH, WE GOT GOOD

DENTISTS HERE IN TROY" one time, I heard it a thousand times during the three years I played for Coach Creel.

- Pete Jenkins – long-time defensive guru who left Troy for LSU for ten years, then moved on to the NFL for another twenty years. Coach Jenkins, who was always looking for an edge for his players, approached me one day at practice and said, "Spillers, what makes you so goddamn mean?" I said, "I guess it's because I was brought up on the other side of the tracks, Coach." He thought for a minute then said, "Damn if I ain't gonna move some of my linemen over there today."

- Doc Anderson - the greatest trainer who ever lived. Also an equally adept track coach. Doc took pity on no one, but healed all! Almost a walking, talking historian of Troy Athletics from the '60s until today. He is a special man!

- Mike Amos - the heart and soul of what support for Troy University athletics is all about. Mike has been a supporter and alumni leader in growing Troy athletics into the 2000s from the '60s, where it all began. Mike is famous in my family for telling my kids when they were teenagers, "Your dad used to be one of the meanest linebackers to ever play at Troy, but look at him now. He looks like a school teacher."

- The Ladies of This Time Period in My Life:

Julie Clark - was an absolute beauty from Jacksonville, Florida. Not only beautiful on the outside, but the inside as well. As with a lot of women during this time in my life, I figured out how to "blow it" with Julie by dumping her because I thought she was immature. When I decided that she was mature enough for me, she told me to shove it! As was the case with most women of quality, I never got a second chance. Even though I begged and pleaded, she would see me occasionally, but would not take me back.

Shelly Centers - God! I could and probably will write a book just on Shelly Centers alone. Shelly was a beautiful, tall redhead who had only one speed when she was drinking . . . full speed! And be damned anything or anybody who would cross her or get in her way. She got me into so many fights, I can't count them all. Once as I was being "temporarily banned" from Friday's by the manager for getting in three fights in one month, he said, " Gary, I know these fights weren't your fault, but you may want to consider changing girlfriends." Shelly was as sweet and loving as any one person could be—most of the time. I just had to keep her out of bars and public drinking places in general.

Stacy Evans – the prettiest girl God ever put on this planet! Well, the prettiest he ever put next door to me anyway. A former Miss Florida USA and a top-10 contestant in the Miss USA Pageant, she was a down-to-earth good girl. We had a lot of fun, but we were mostly just friends.

Cheryl Petros - what can I say? She was the one that got away. When I look back on our relationship, I realize I blew it! I was in love with her, but I wasn't ready to give up the party life and certainly not ready to commit to a monogamous relationship. That's all she wanted. I couldn't give it. When I got back from my trip, and, ironically, while Nicki from Aspen was visiting me in Atlanta, I found out Cheryl was dating a short, older guy in Atlanta pretty seriously. I was crushed. When I was told about Cheryl and the other suitor, all my thoughts shifted from enjoying Nicki being in town to how fast I could get her back on a plane to Colorado. I needed time to myself to plan how I would handle this situation with Cheryl. The "older guy" was a doctor that I sent her to as a patient. Do you think I will ever send that piss-ant another referral? My feeling at the airport in LA was correct. I never saw her again. She married the doctor.

- THE GREEN PIG – the absolute star of the trip! Never had one minute of trouble with this magnificent steed. Lindy's objections to this fine vehicle at first should have told me something about her intelligence level. The trip ended up being 7,500 miles in length, and I believe that this car burned less than three quarts of oil! It never failed to crank—even on some of those cold Colorado mornings that exploded my champagne bottle. I ended up giving the car away to a couple of high school kids who needed reliable transportation.

Epilogue

It's been two months since I got back from the adventurous road trip. So here I sit at 2:00 a.m., looking out another man's window across another man's swimming pool (albeit an interesting one). Cheryl is gone, out of my life forever. I am still basically broke, although I do now have some income from my job with the mortgage company.

As I play back the tapes of the trip, I wonder: Was it really worth it? Maybe if I hadn't gone, Cheryl would still be with me, or maybe I could have landed a better job. What did I really accomplish? What did I learn? Why in the hell did I do it? How stupid could I have been?

But the lingering, ultimate heart-tugging question that I will always answer in the same positive way is, Would you do it again? The answer is . . . HELL YES, I WOULD! I would saddle up that magnificent steed, the Green Pig, and be gone tomorrow! The sites I saw, the people I met, the stories we told, and the "messes" we got into were priceless. It was a once in a lifetime experience that I will cherish for the rest of my days.

Maybe the Pig and I will see you on another road trip in the future. In this crazy world, you never know what will happen and with whom. As the Lone Ranger used to say before he rode off into the sunset, "Hi-yo, Pig! Away!"